This Book Belongs To:

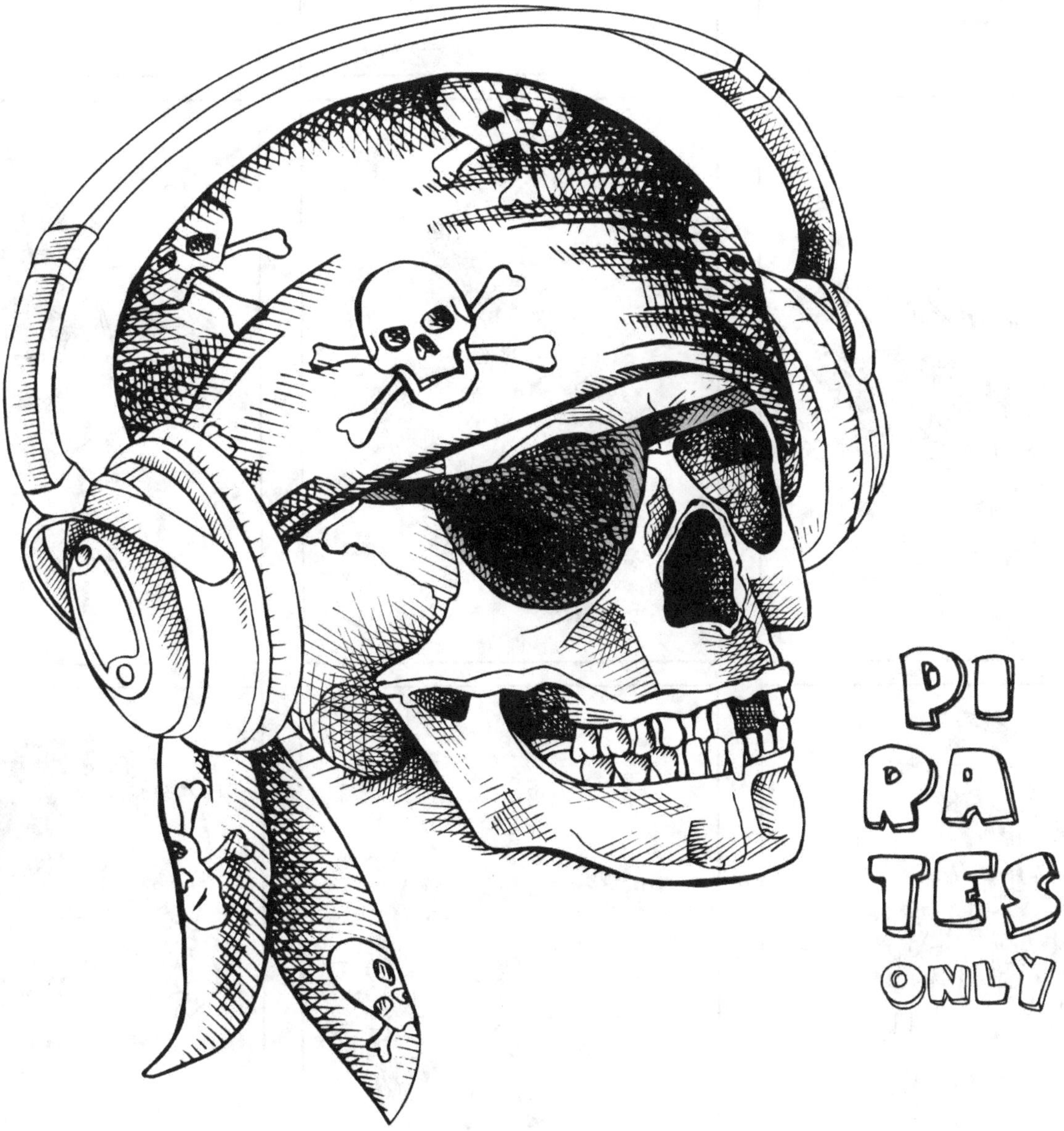

_____

PI
RA
TES
ONLY

Preview of Coloring Pages

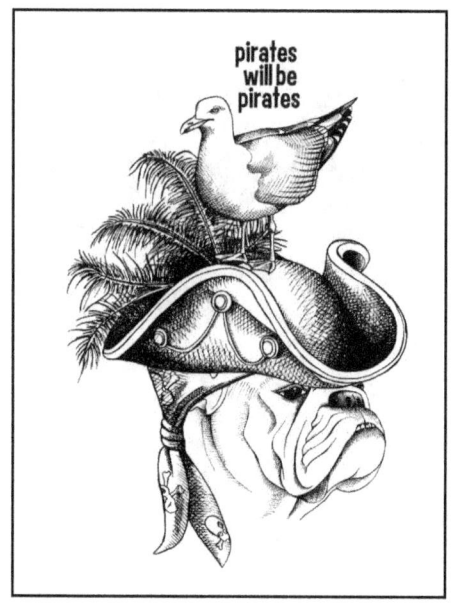

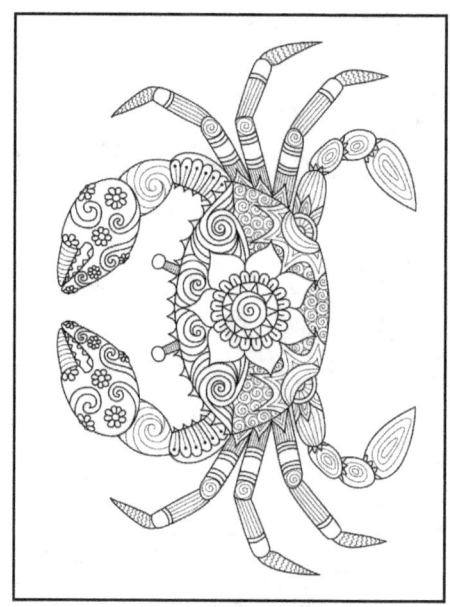

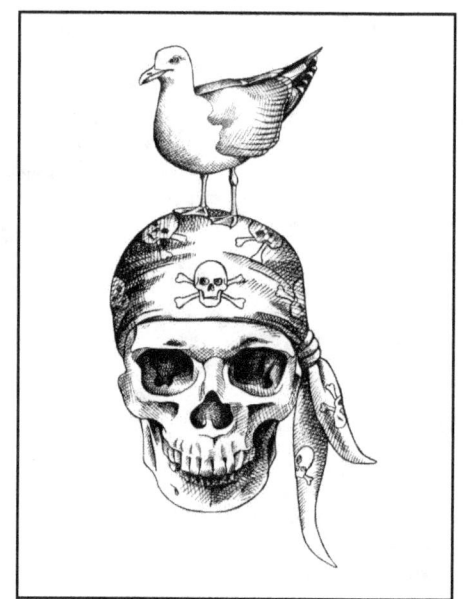

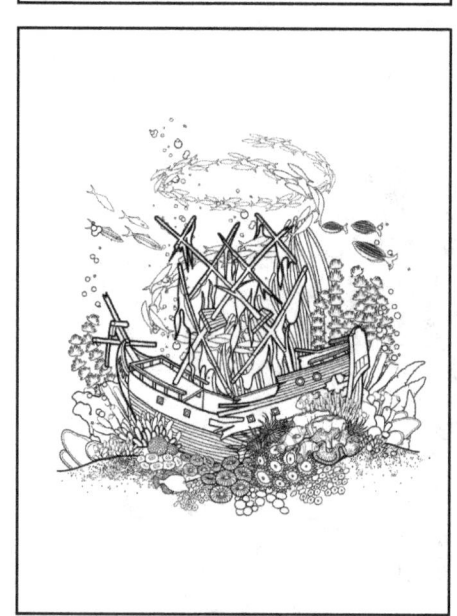

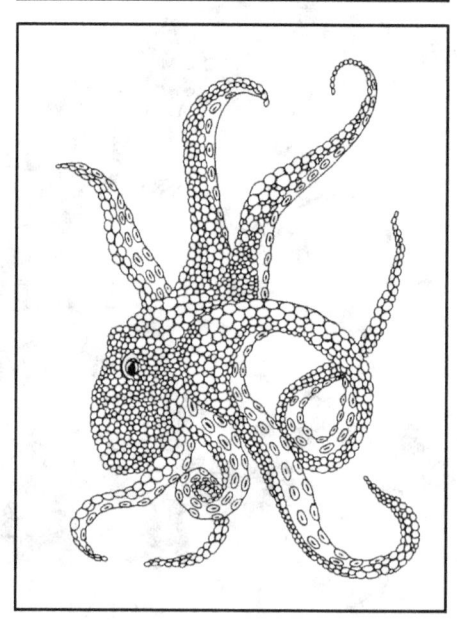

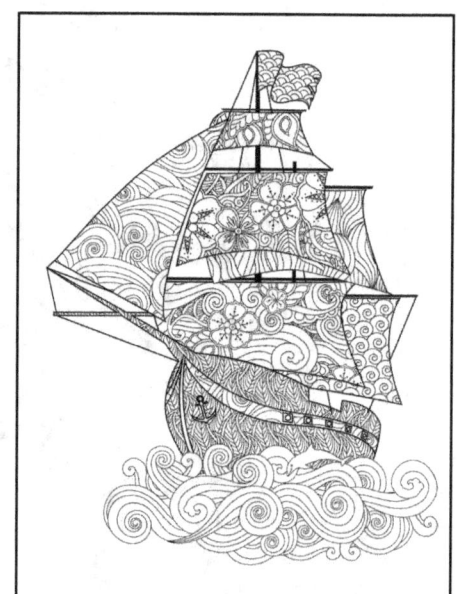

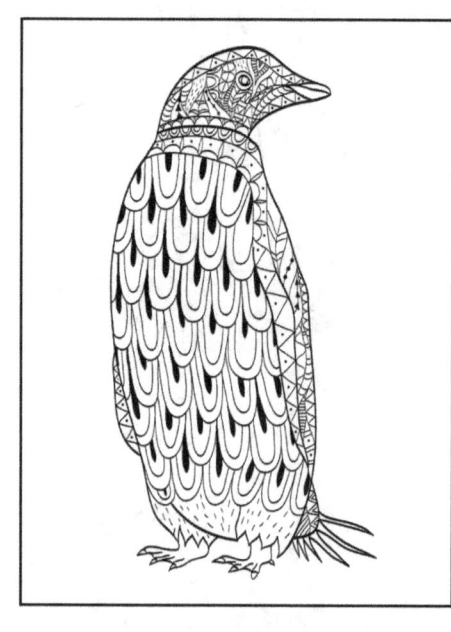

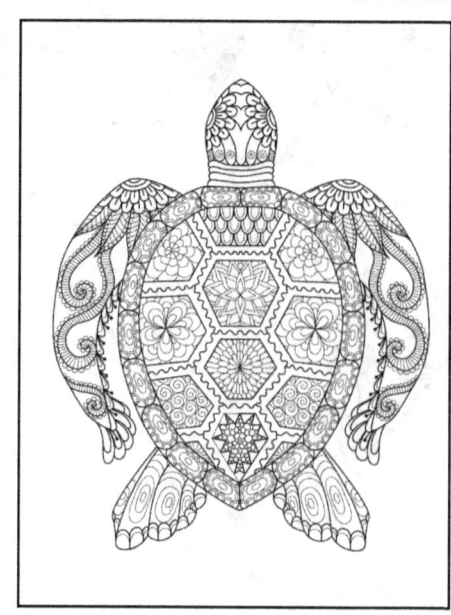

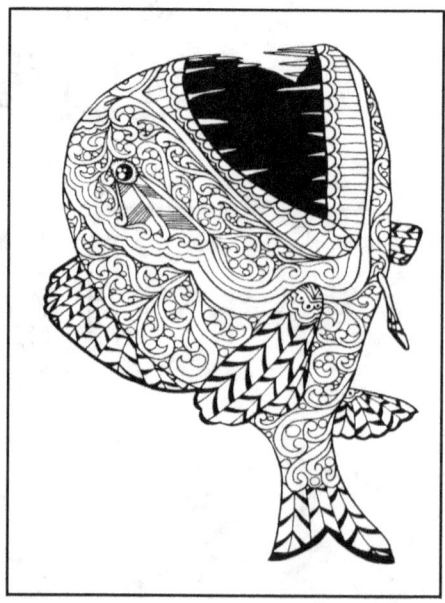

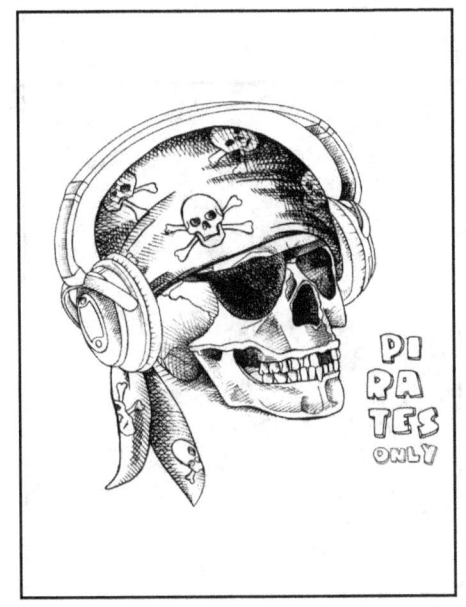

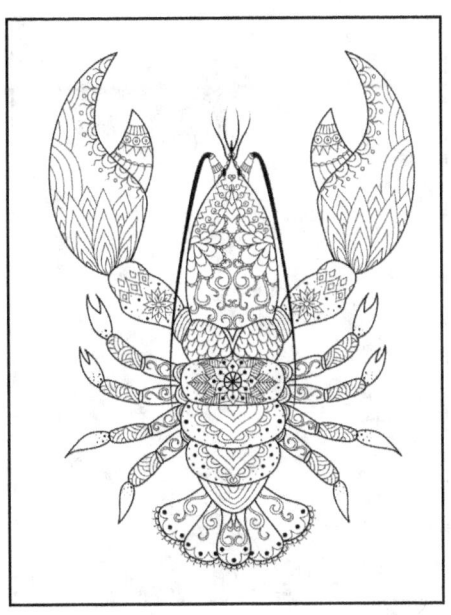

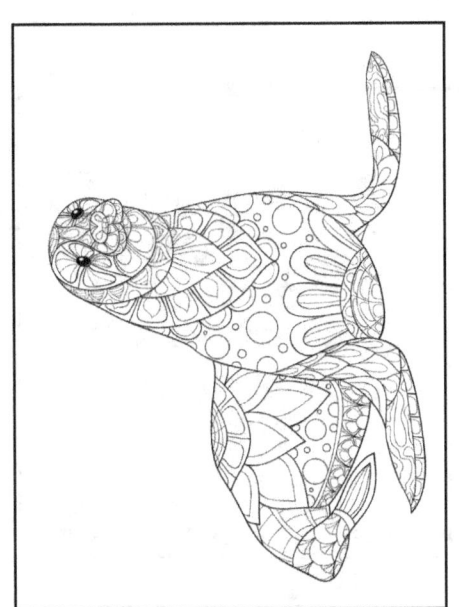

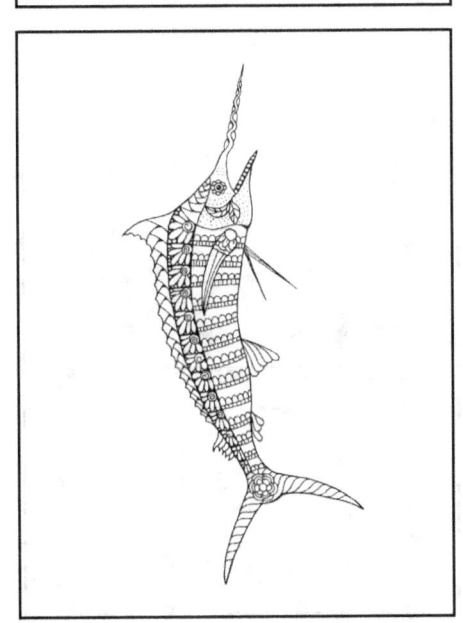

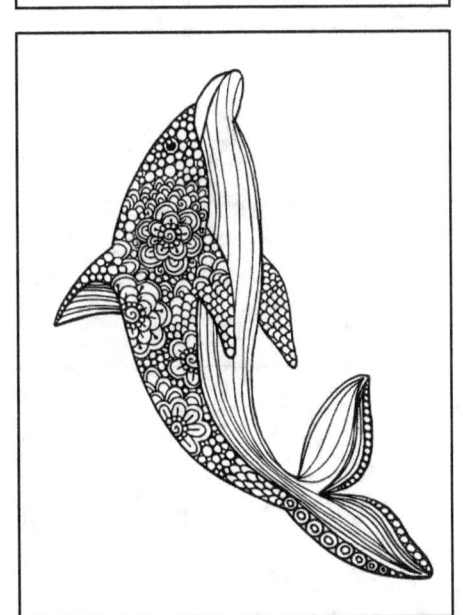

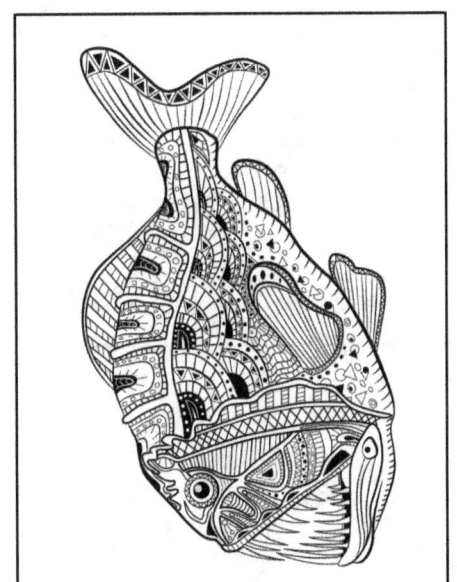

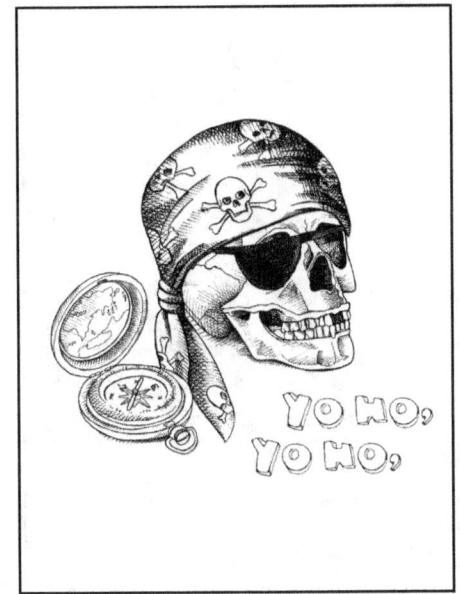

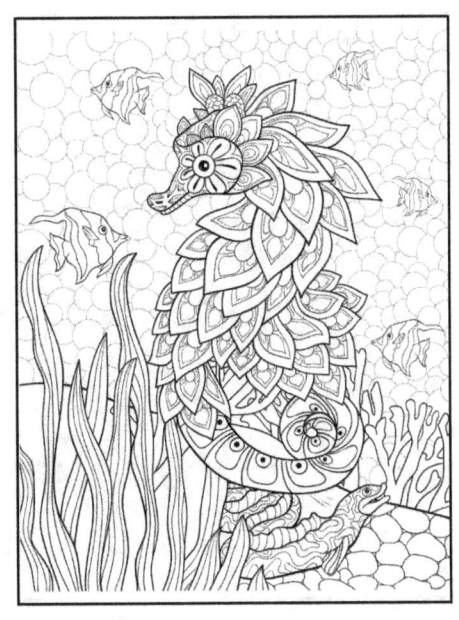

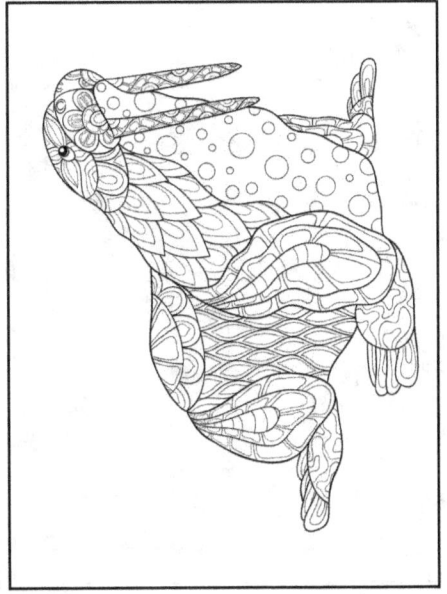

Preview of Coloring Pages

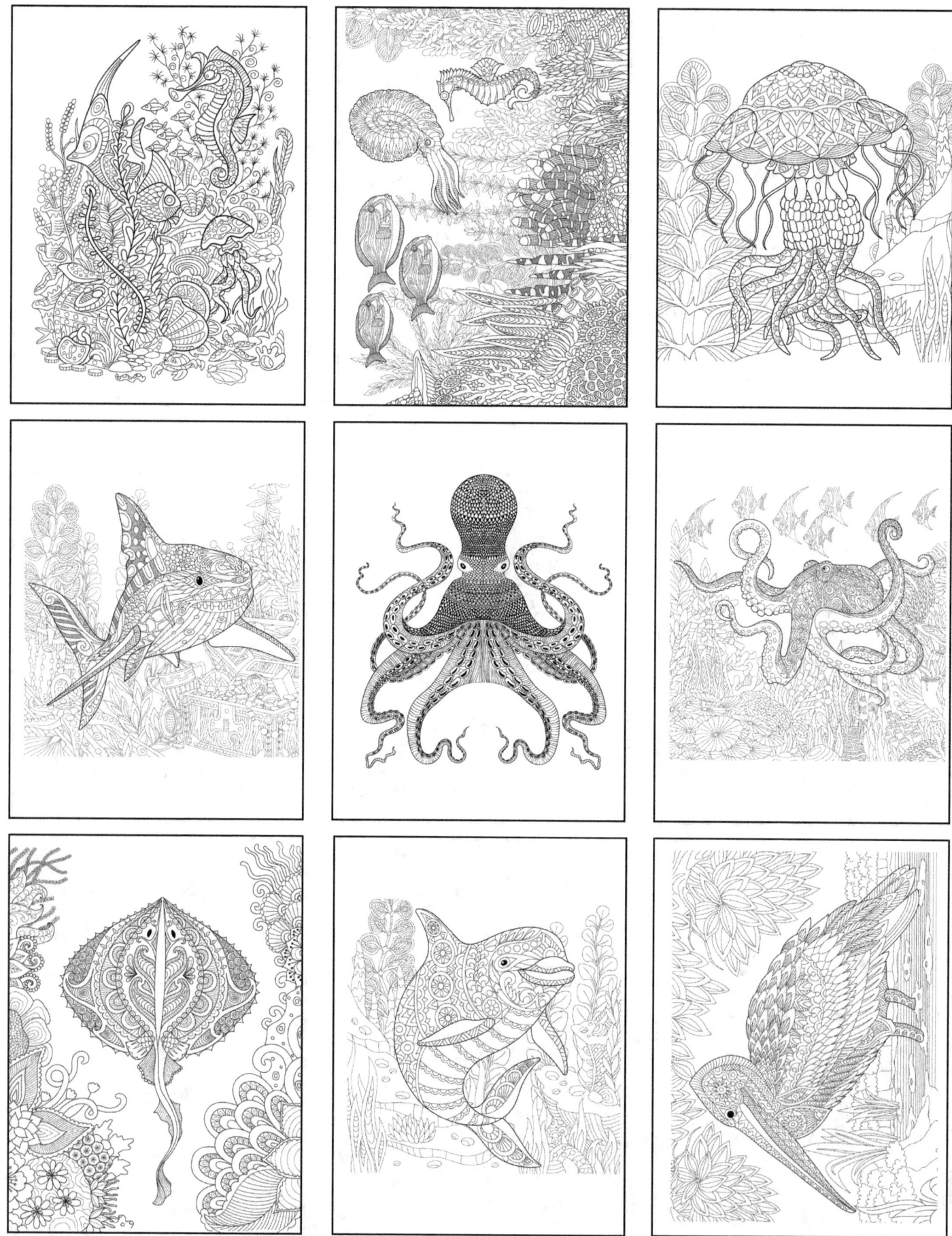

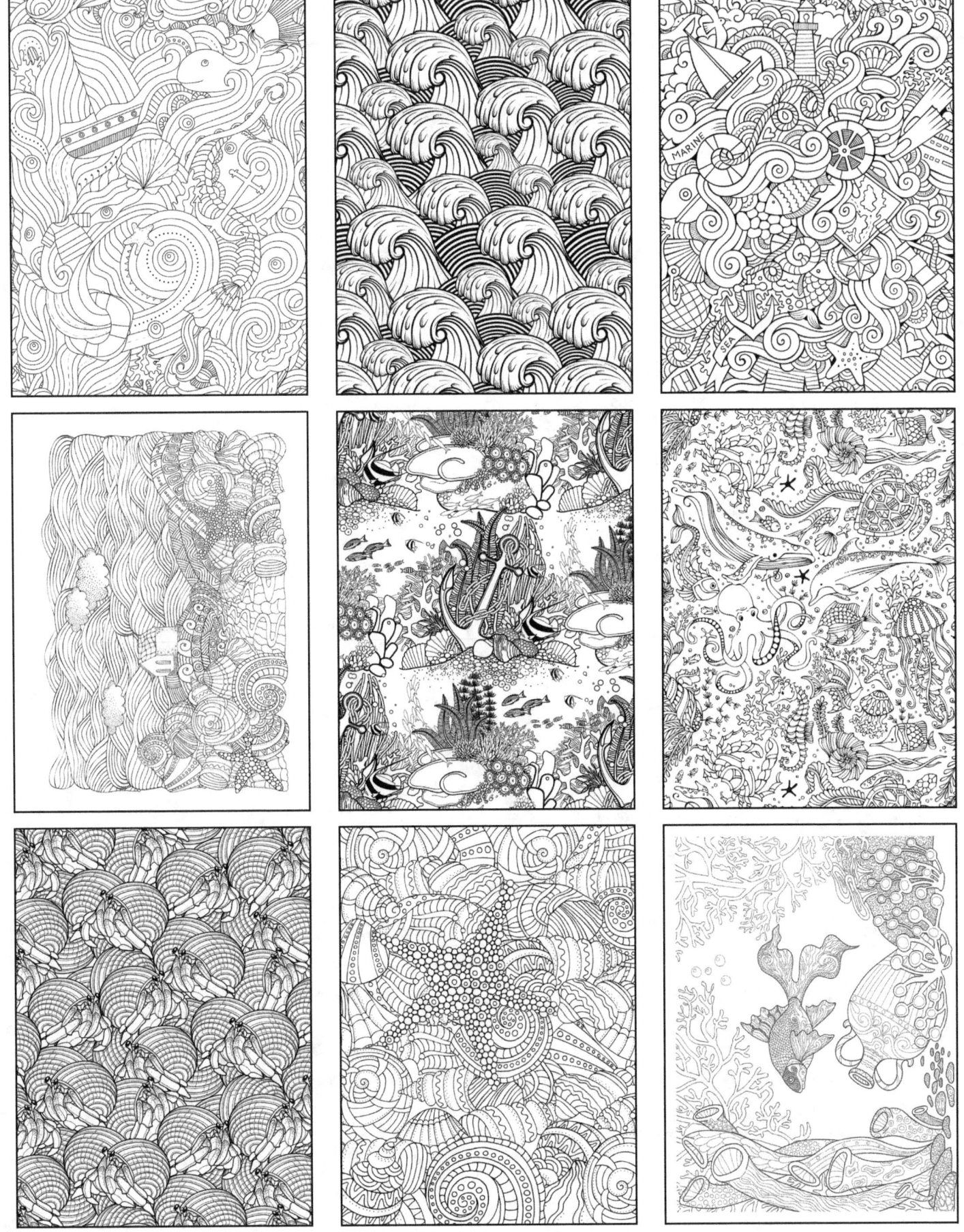

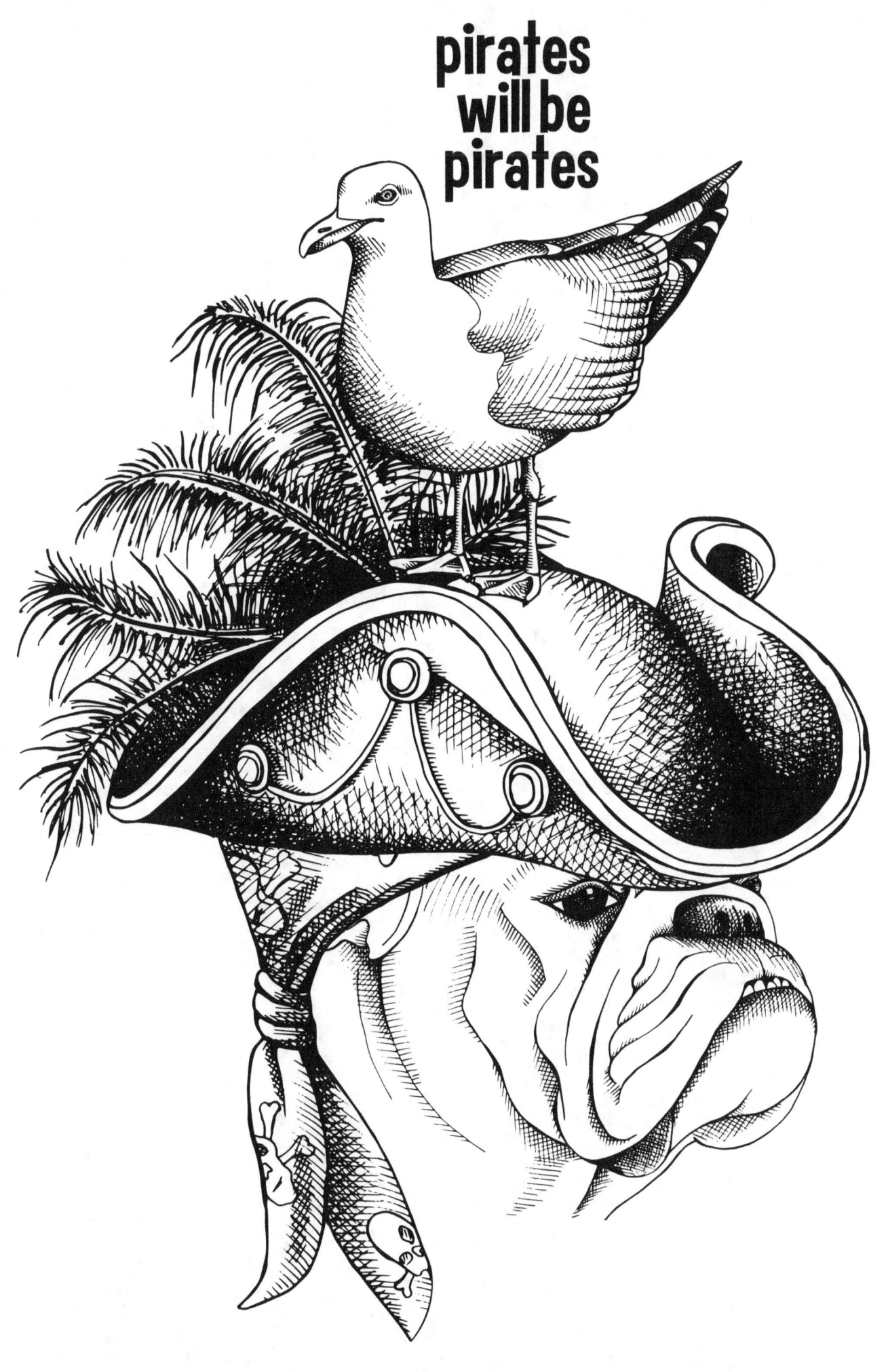

pirates
will be
pirates

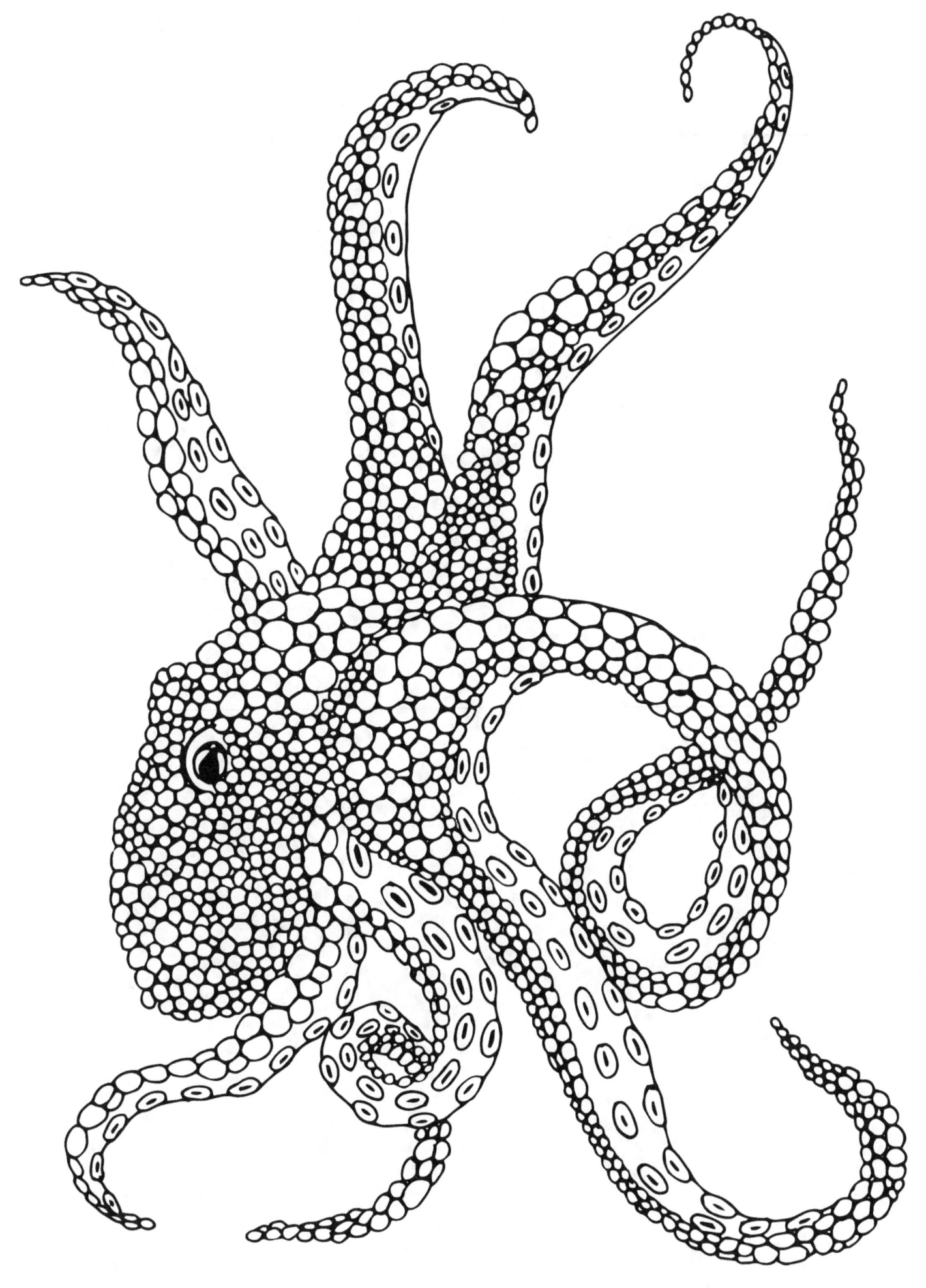

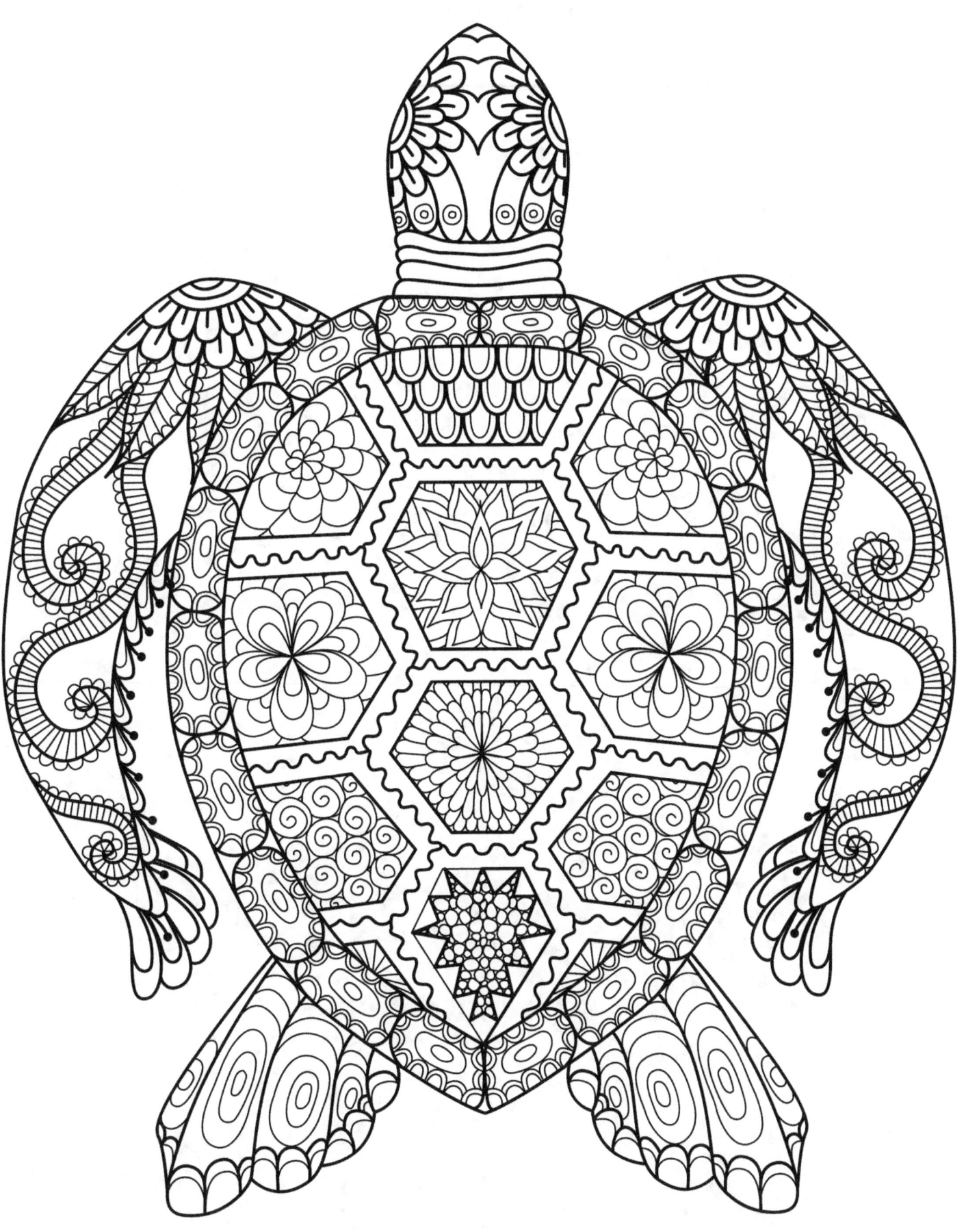

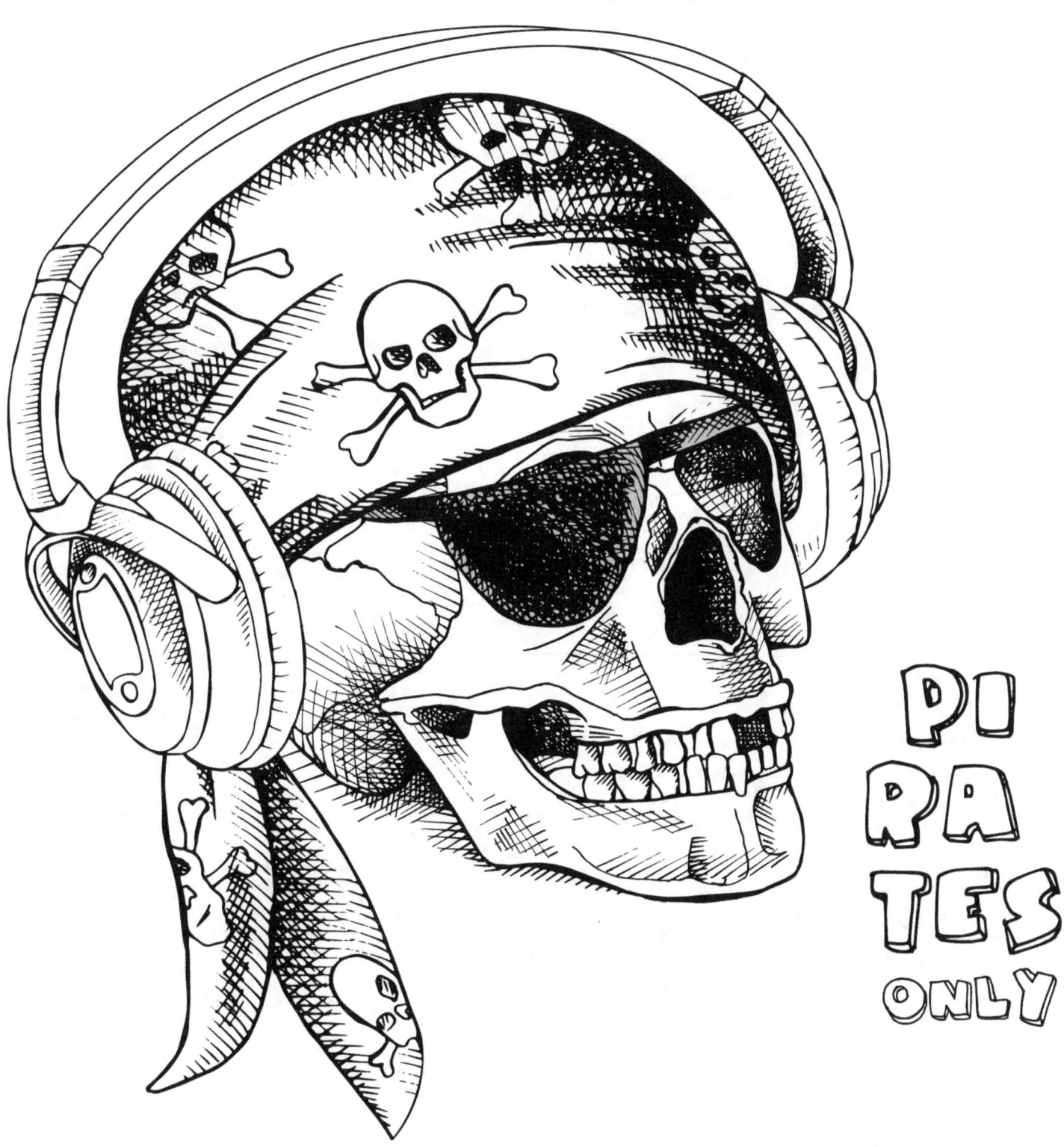

PI
RA
TES
ONLY

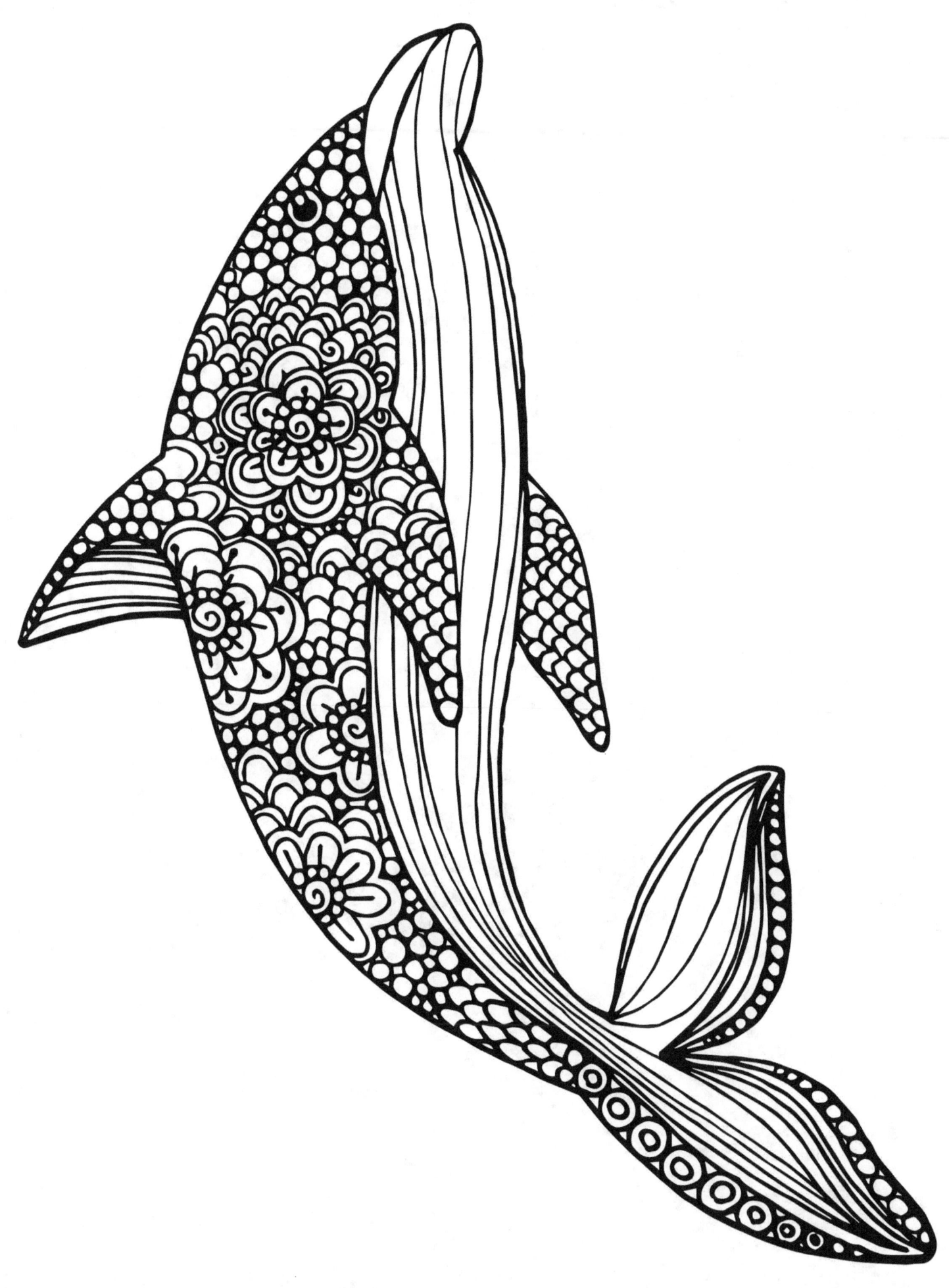

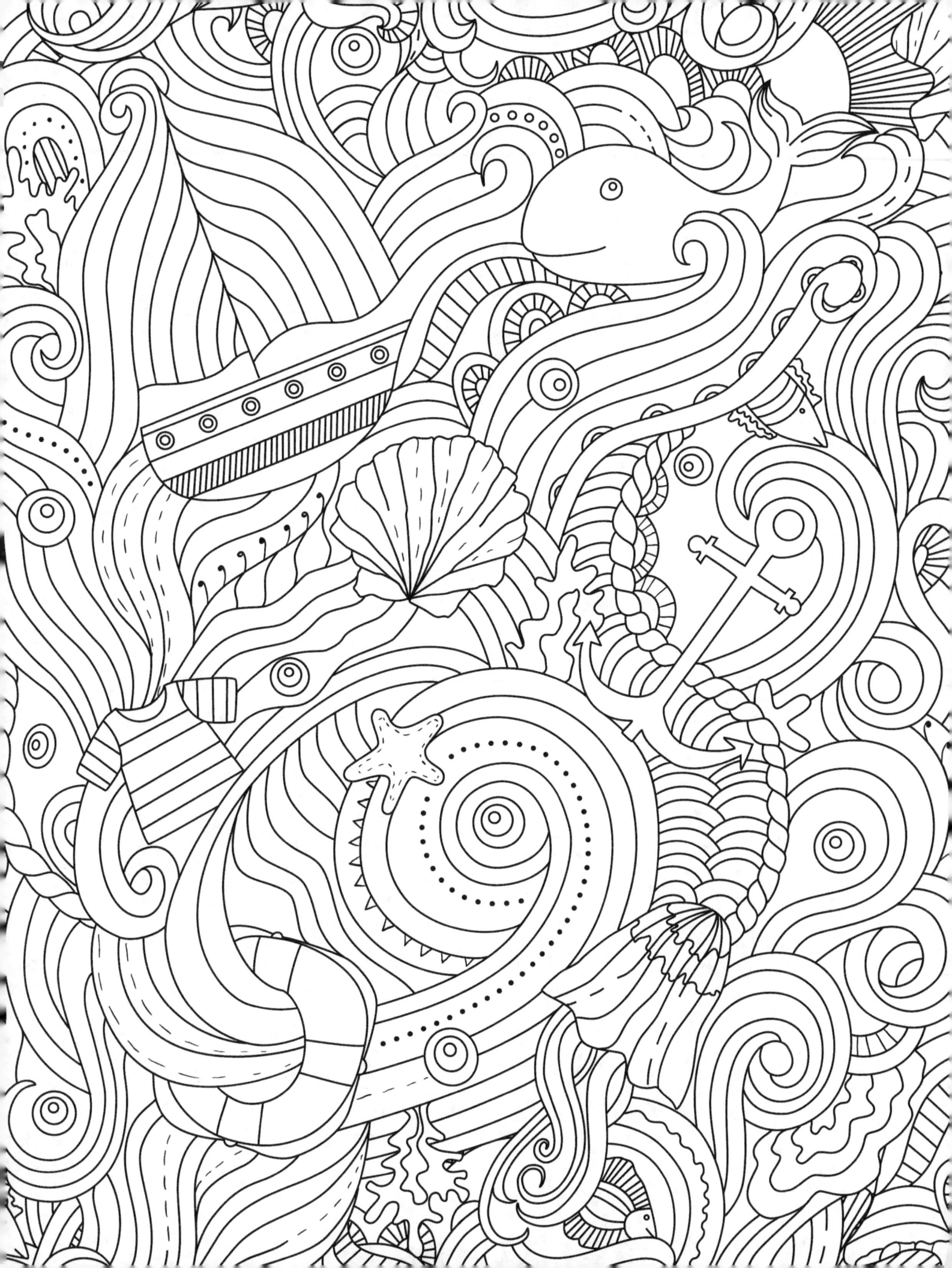

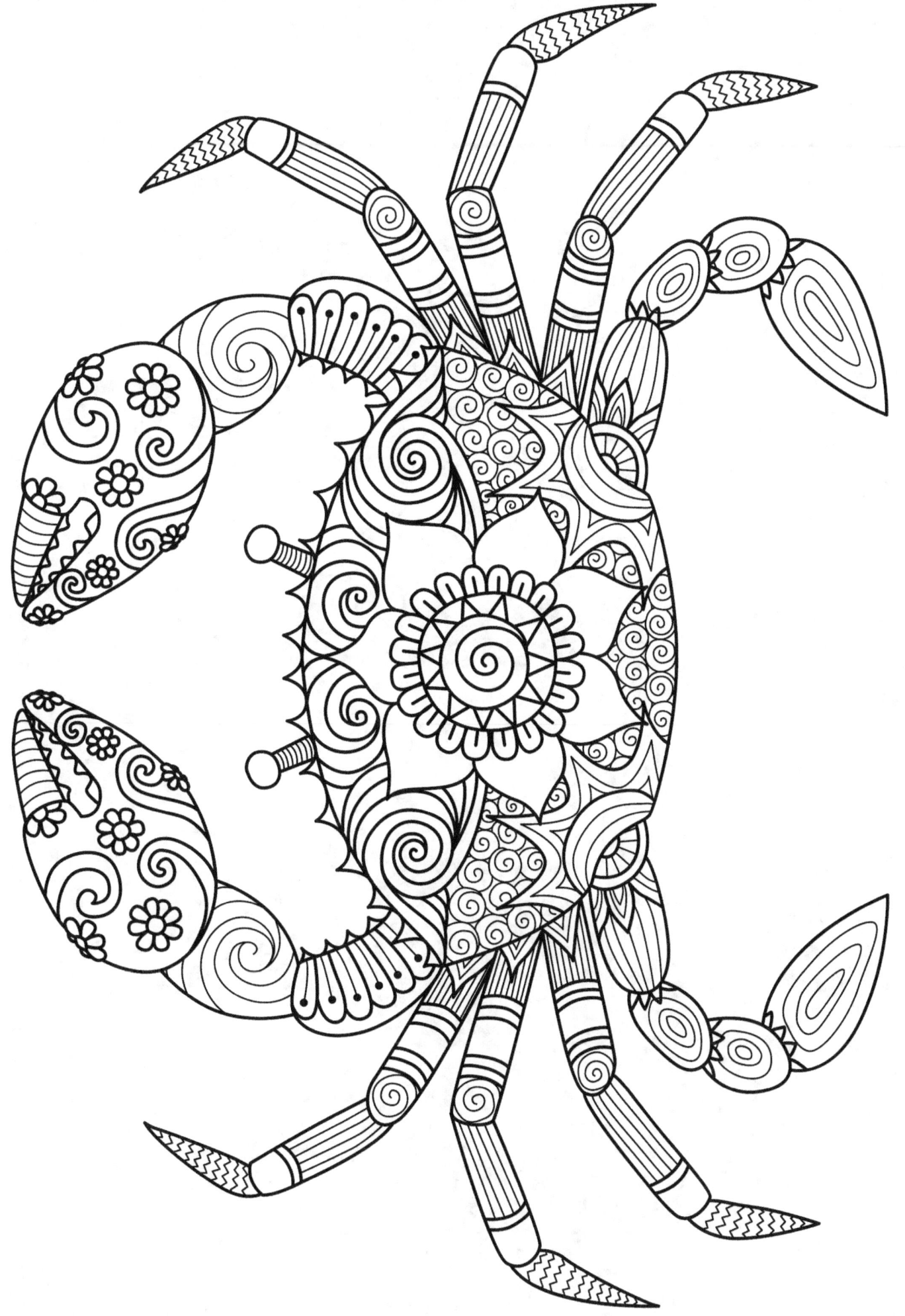

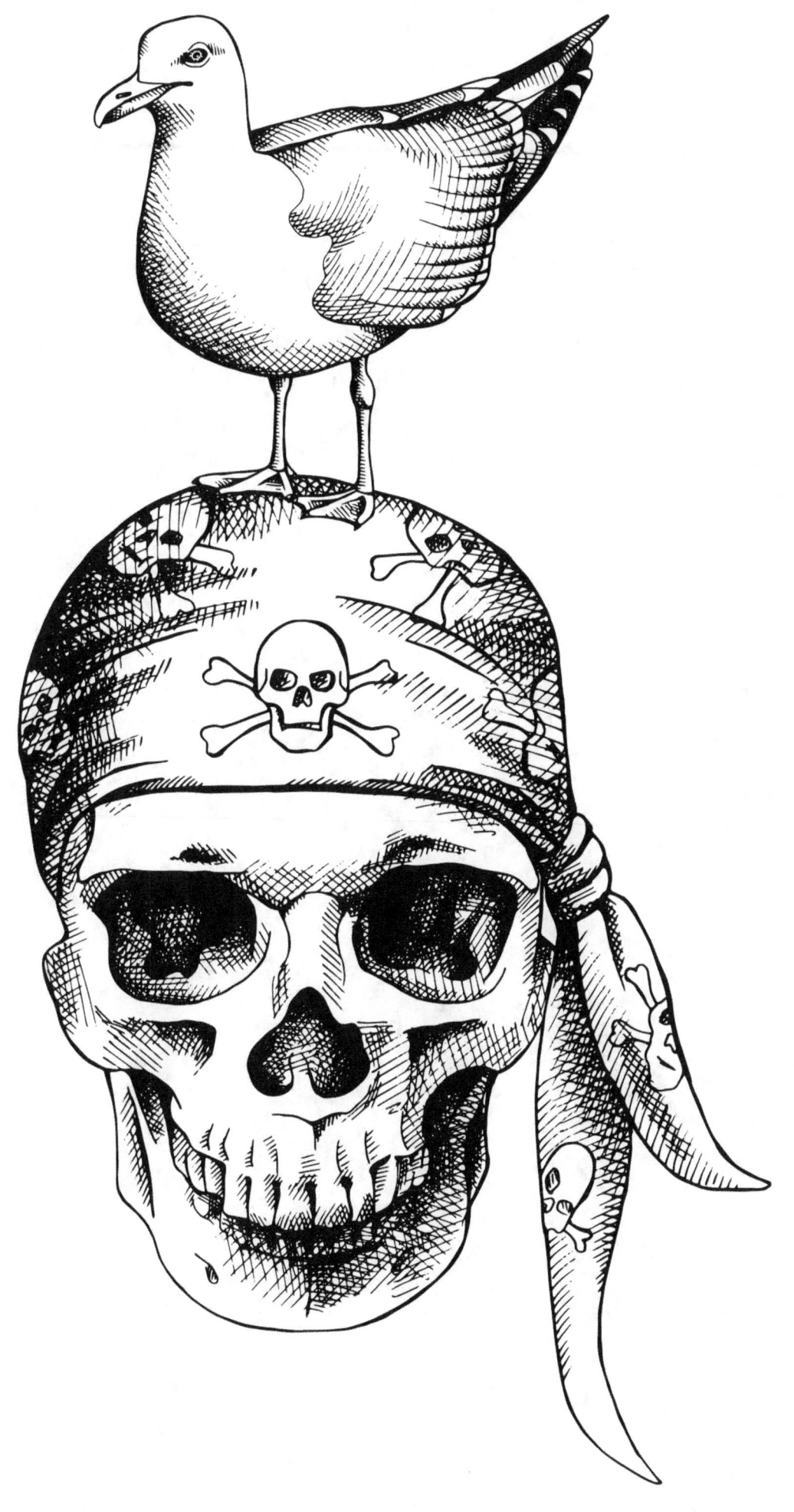

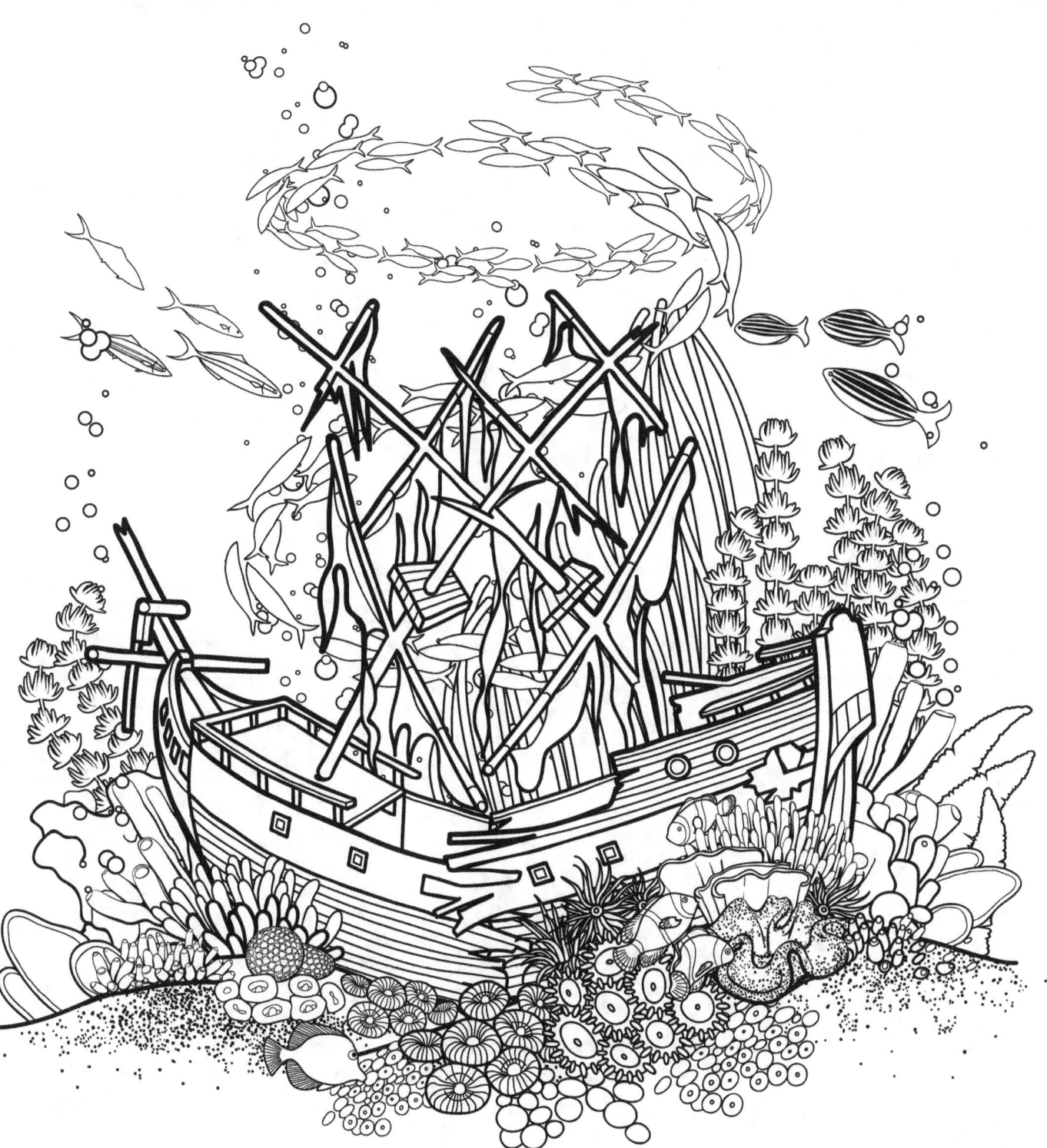

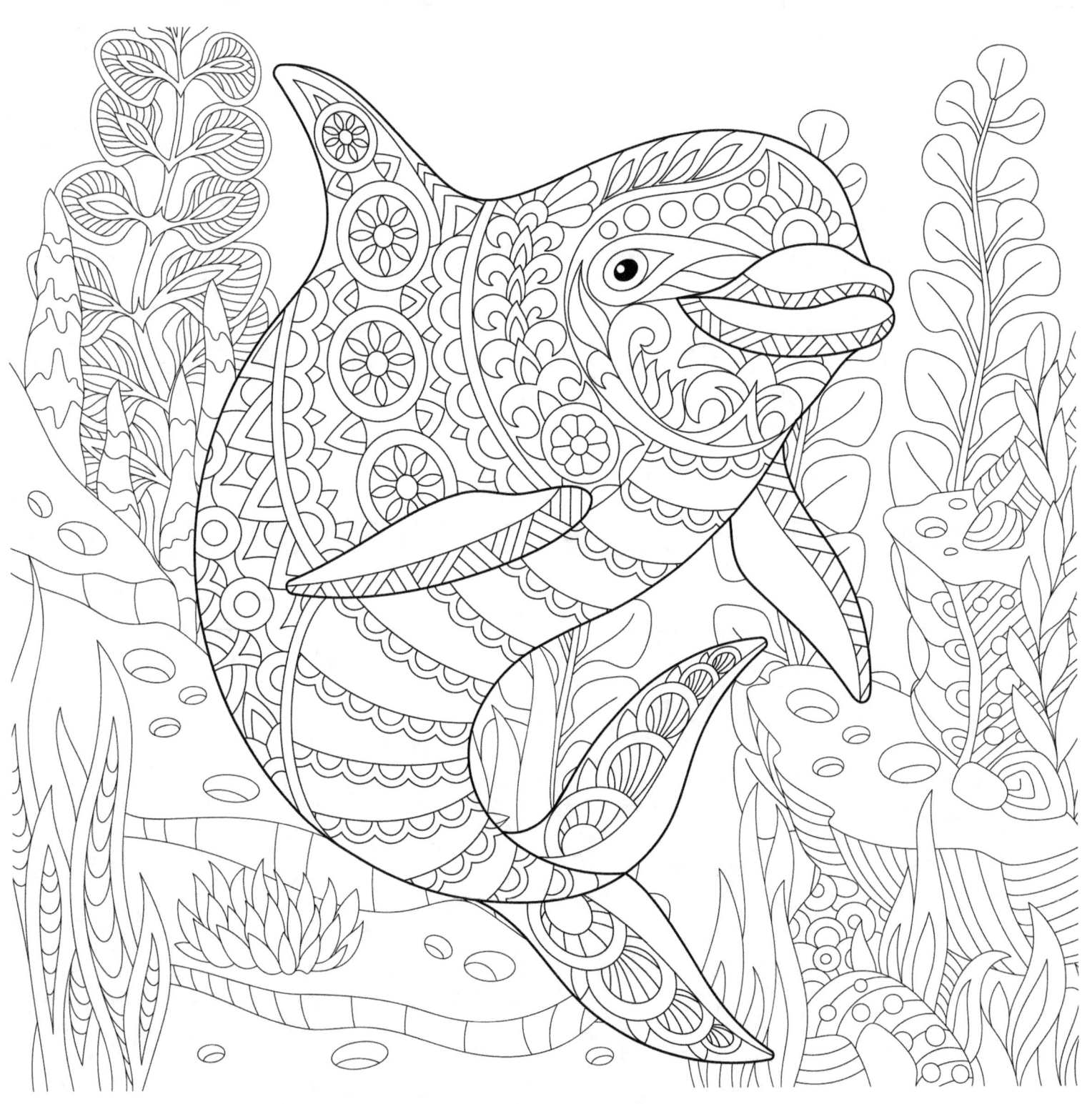

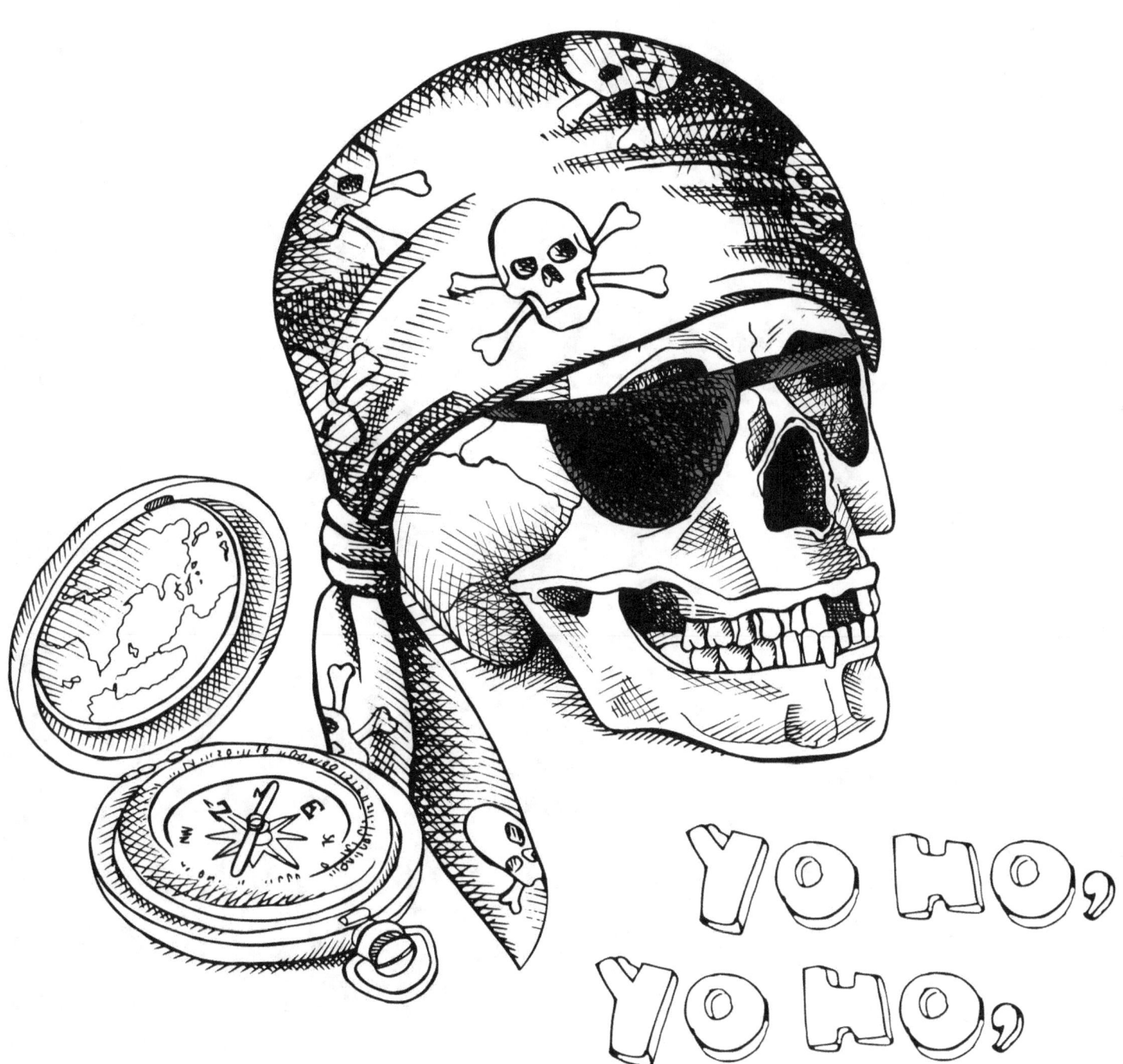

YO HO,
YO HO,

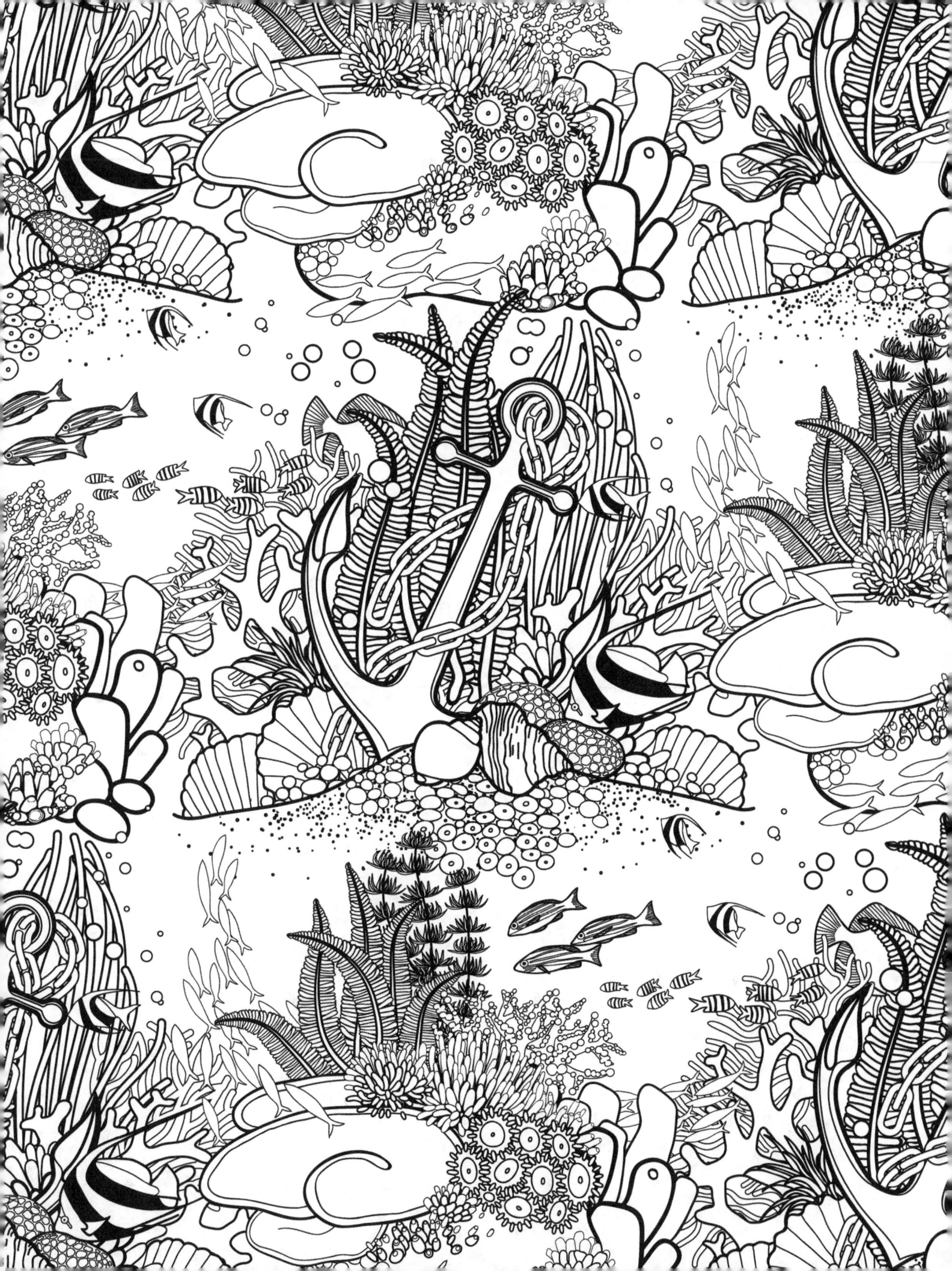

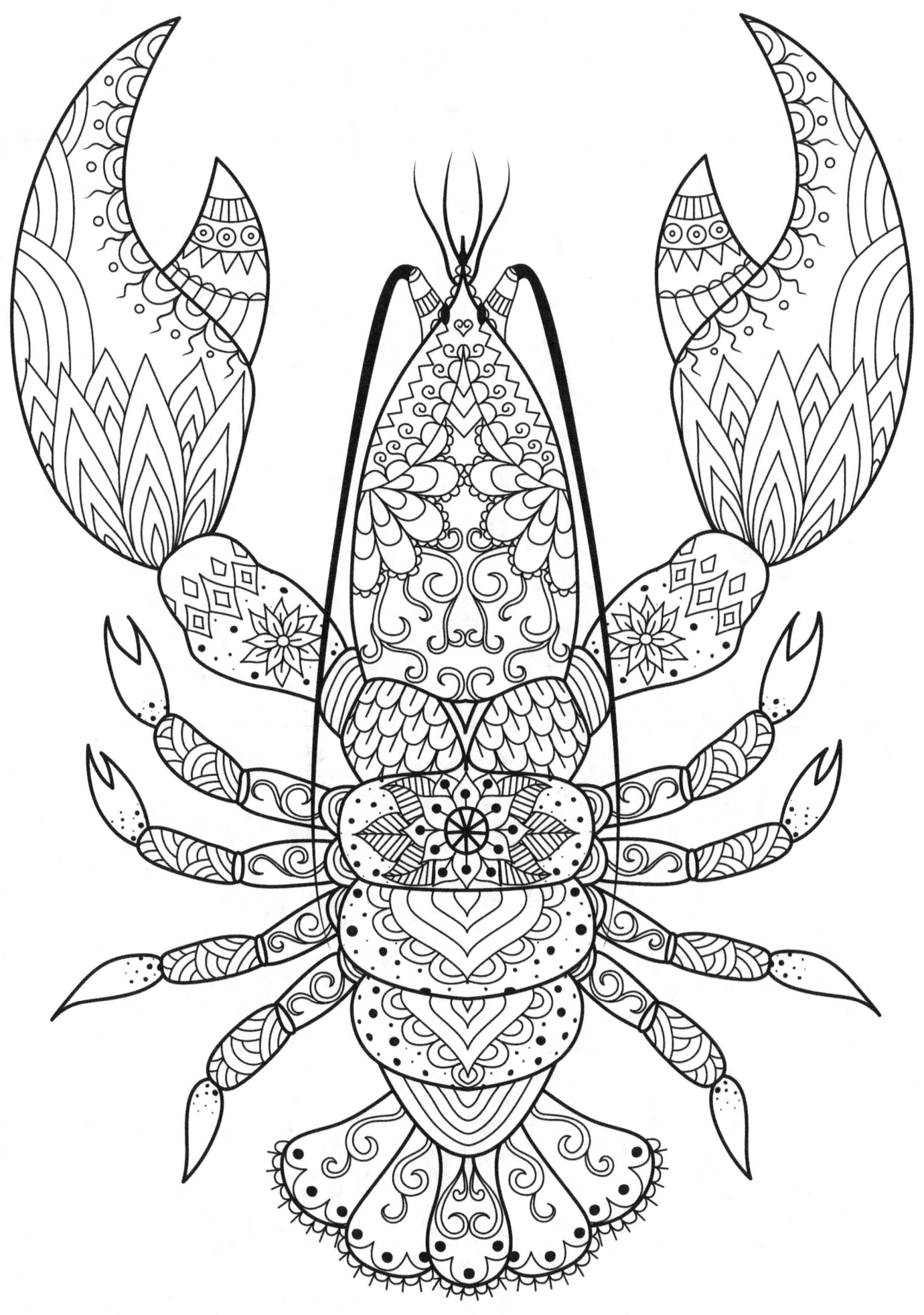

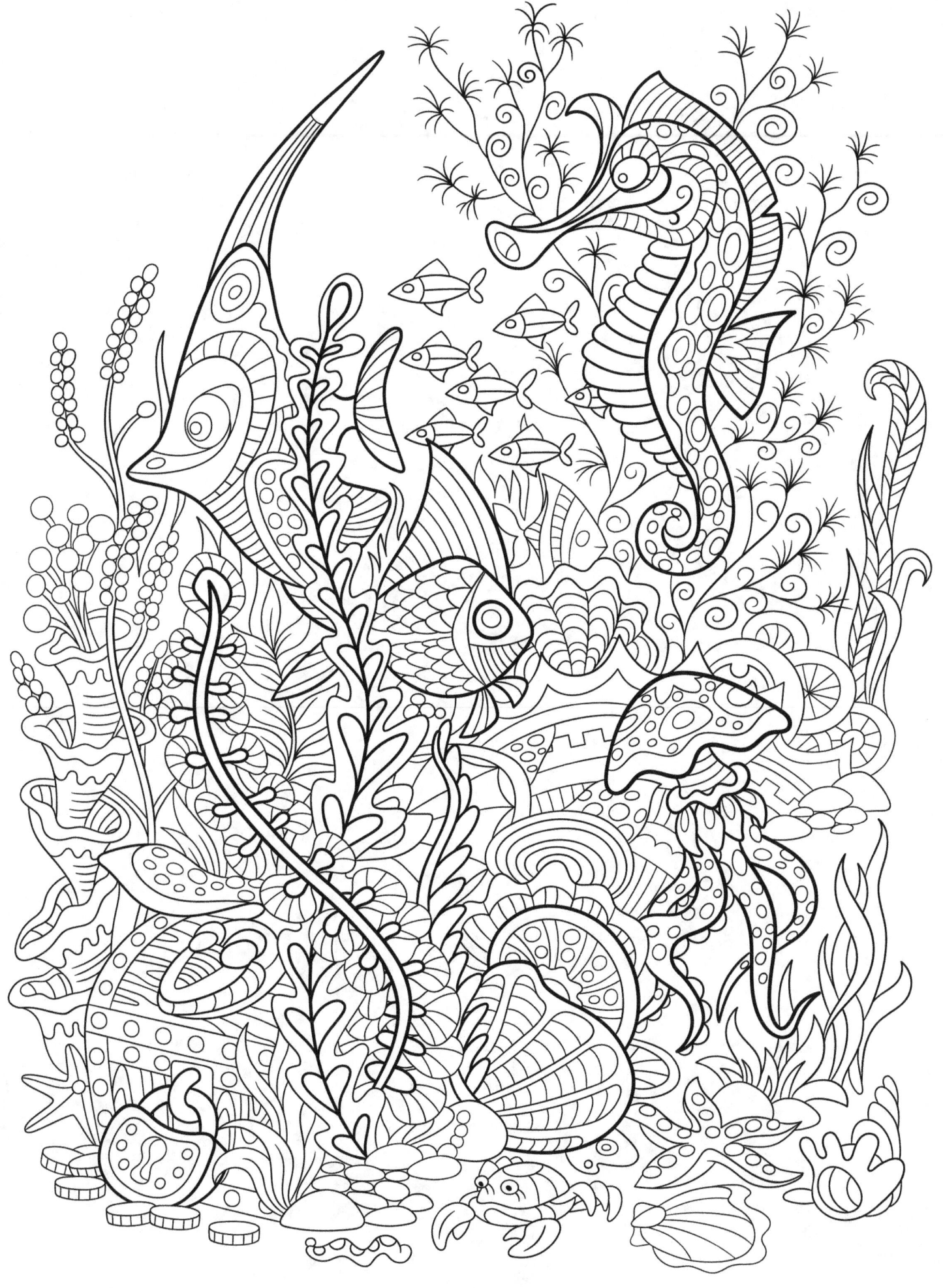

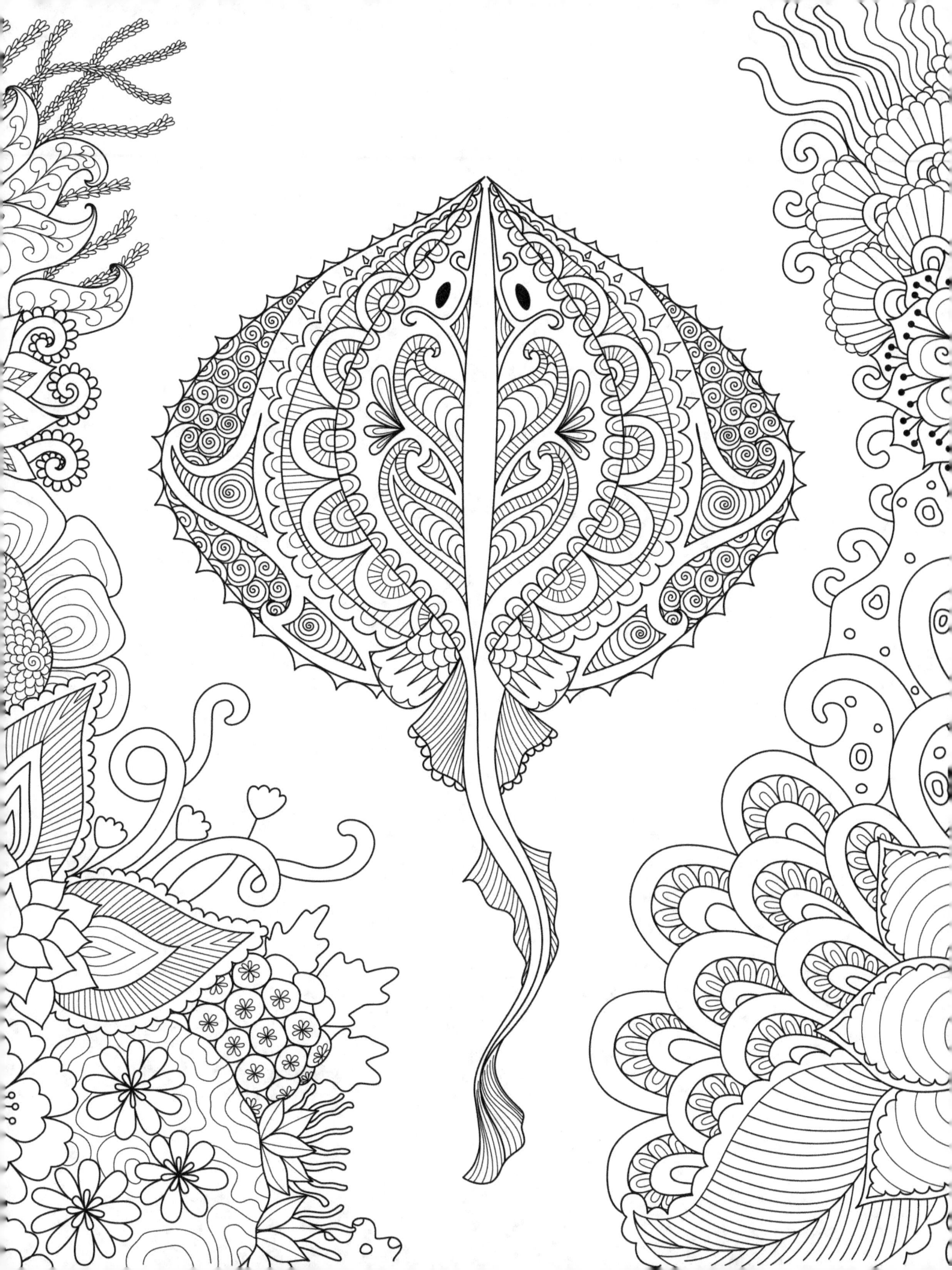

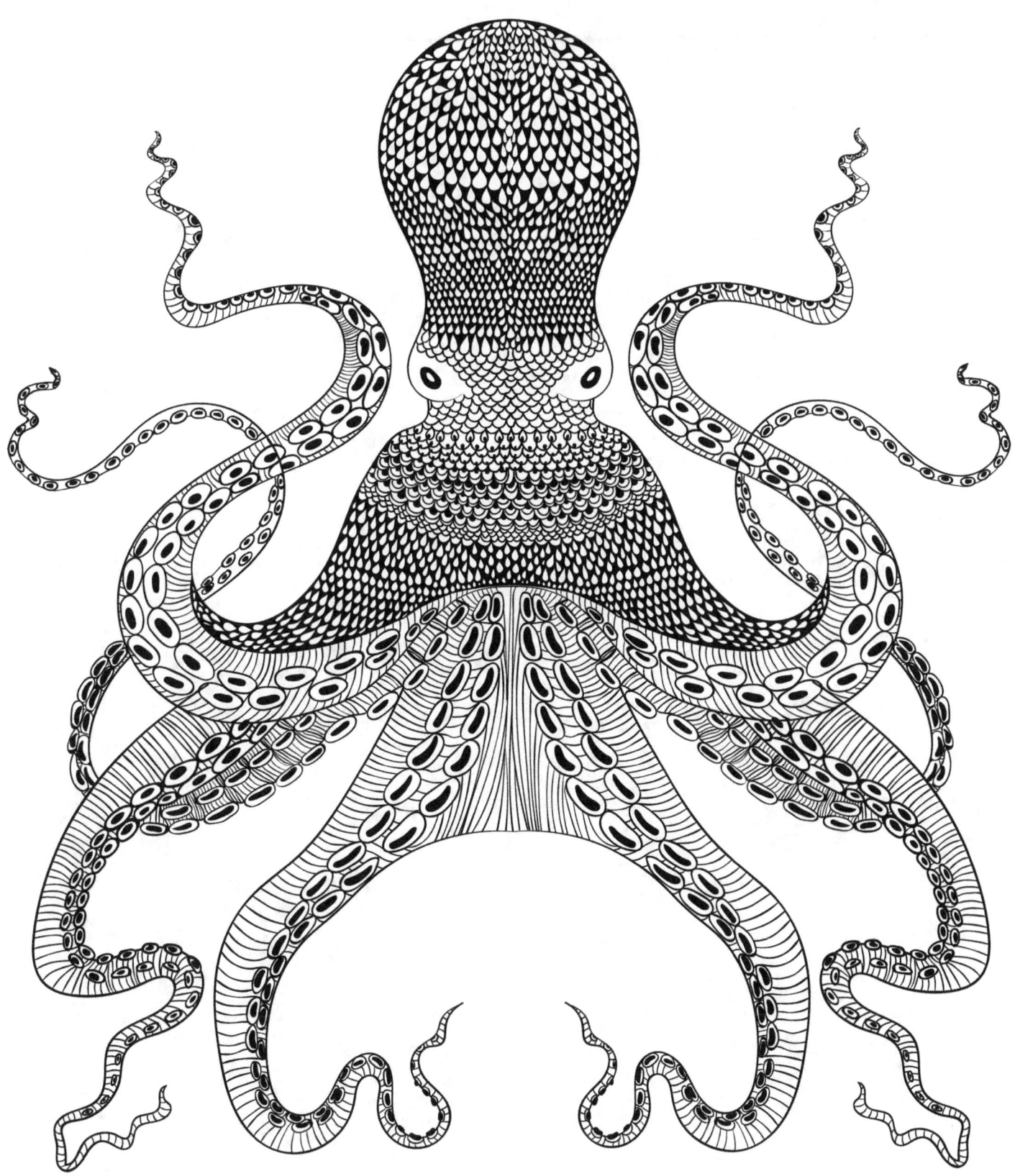

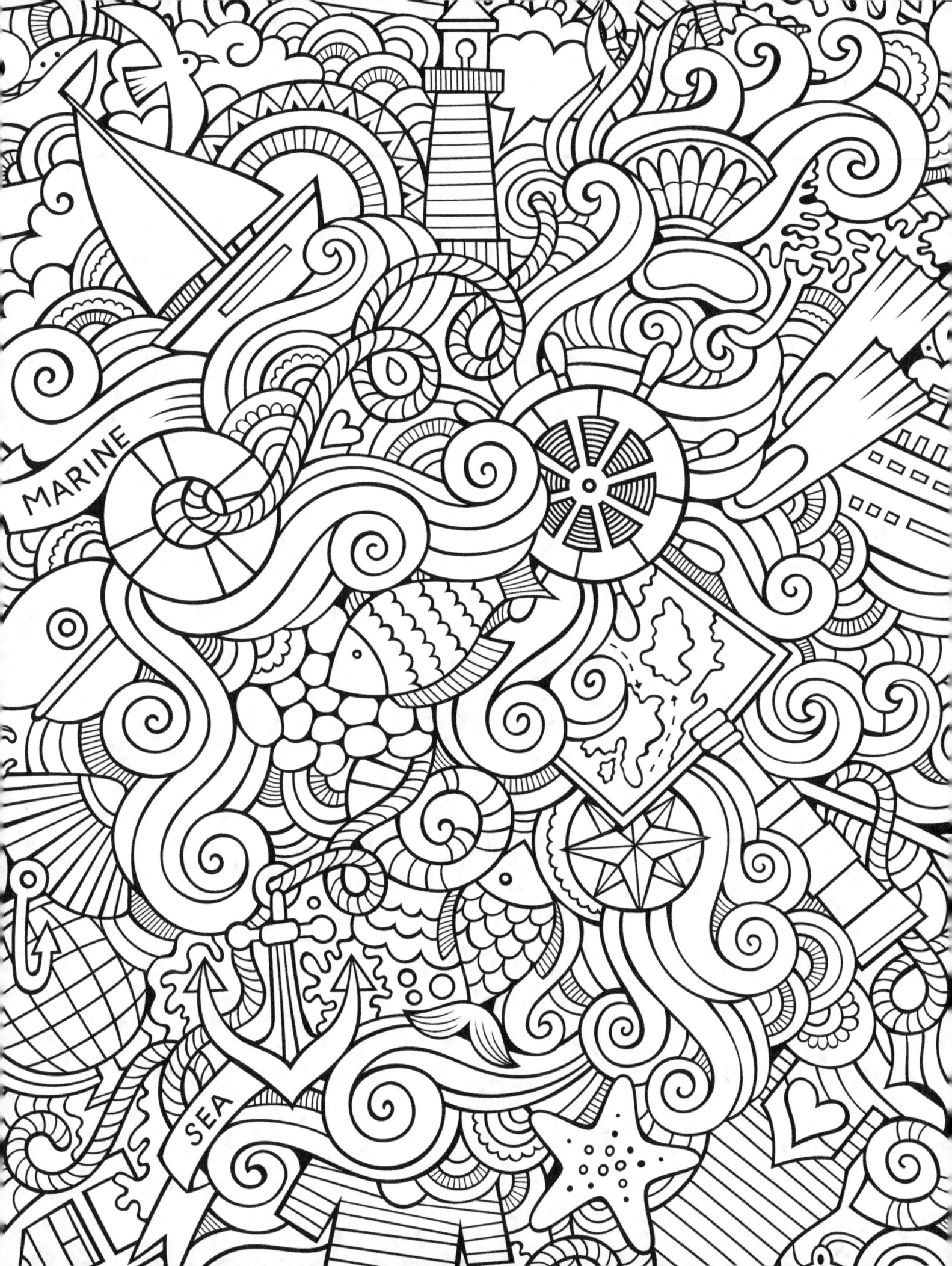

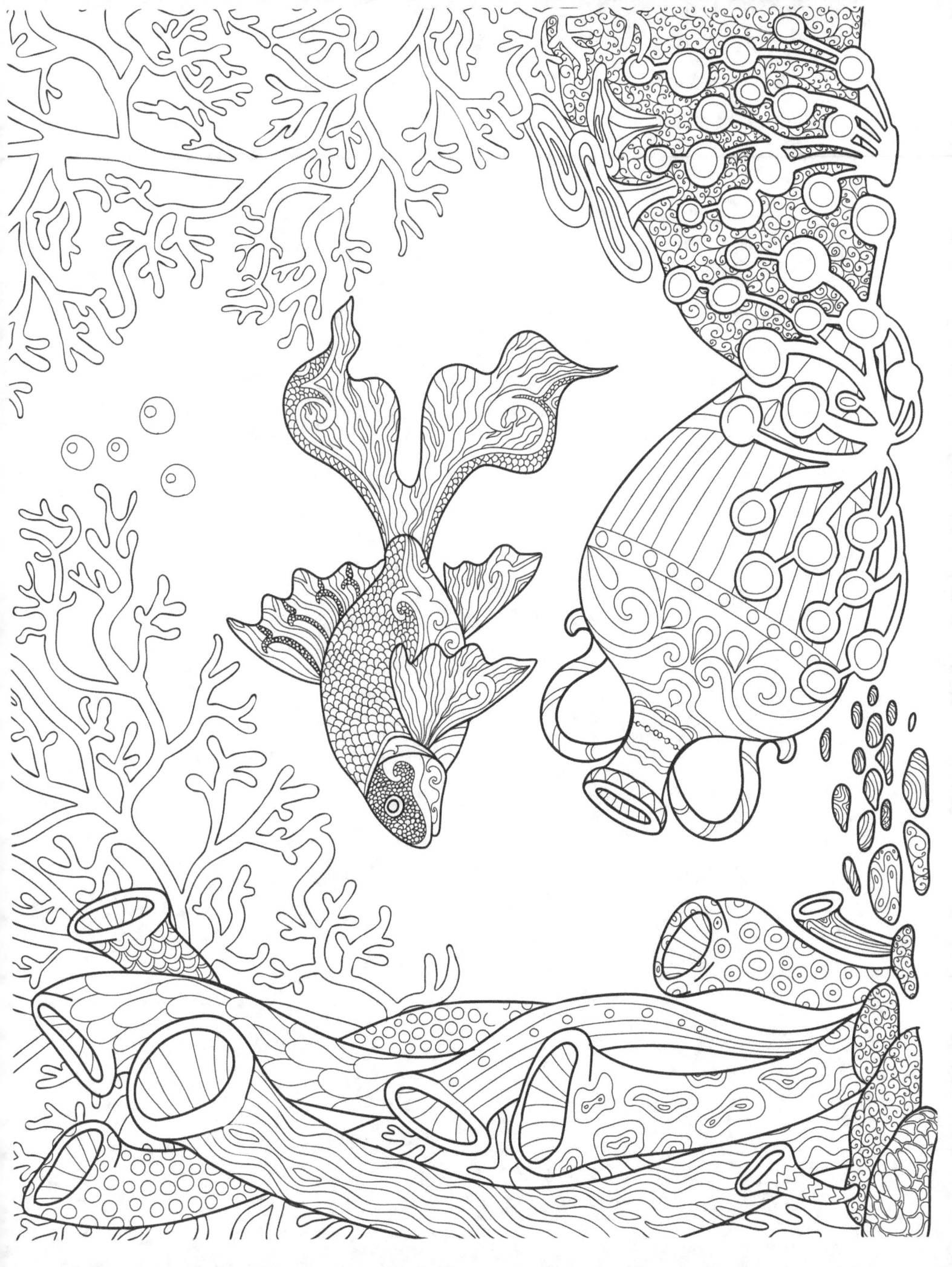

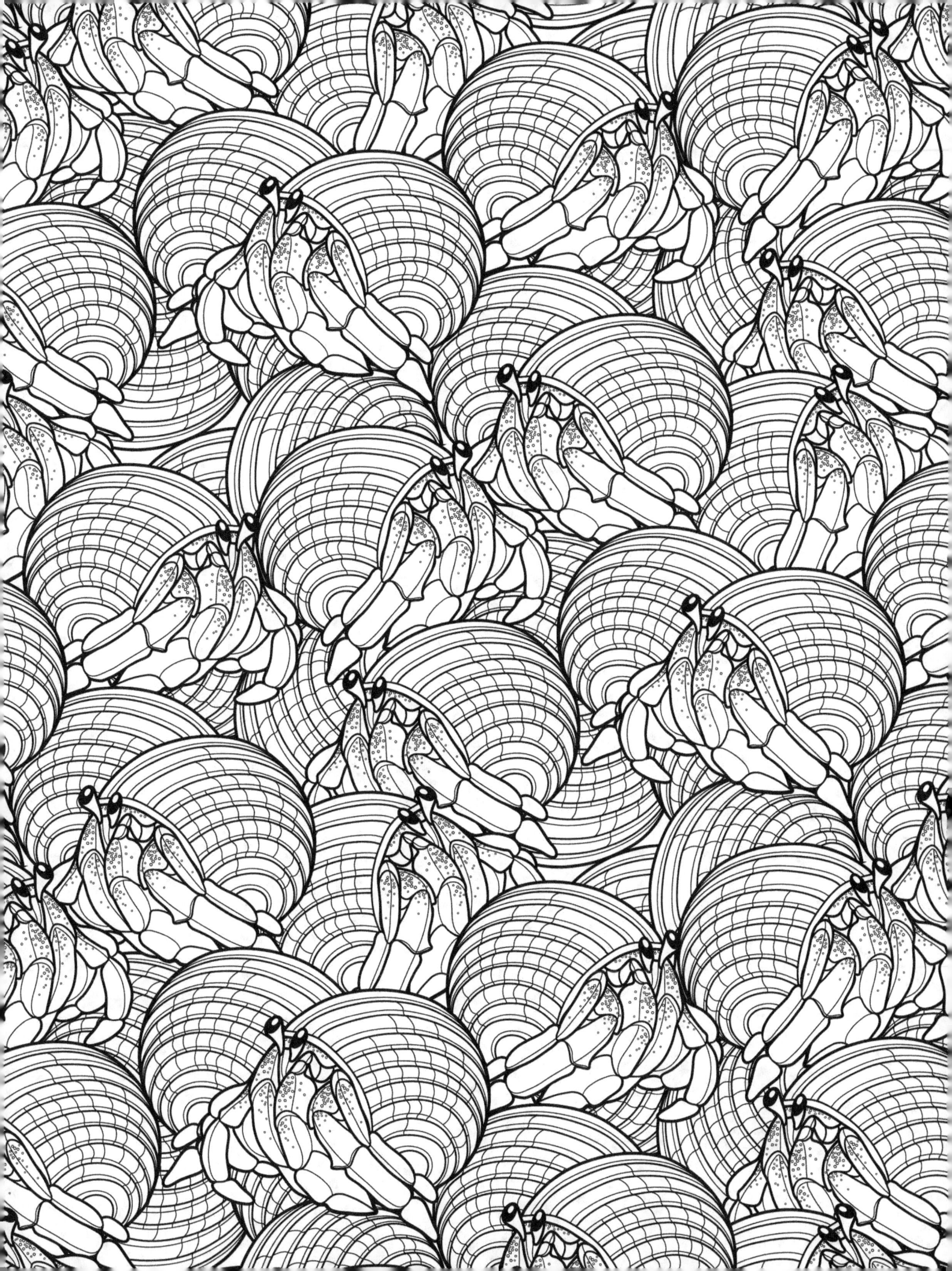

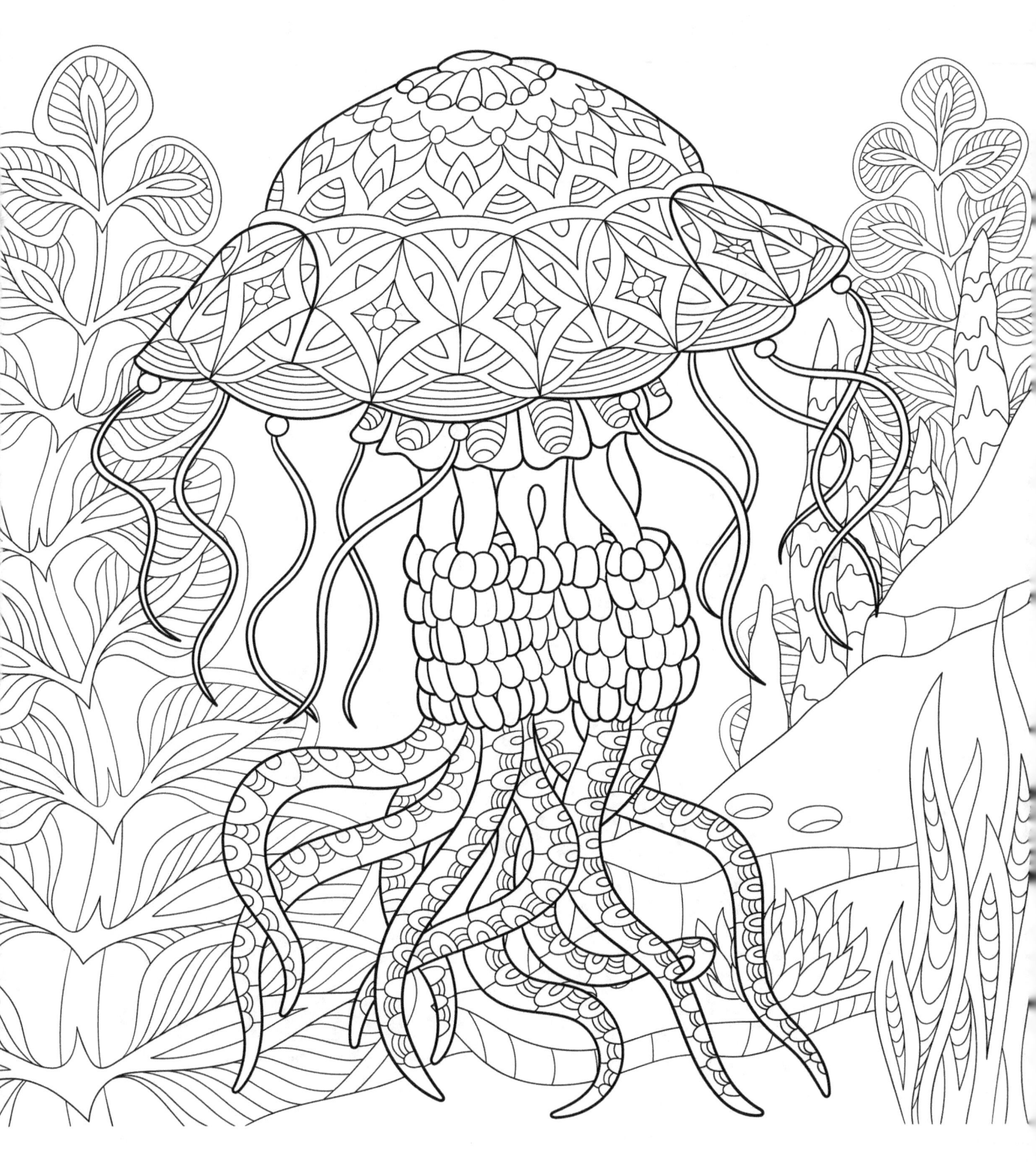

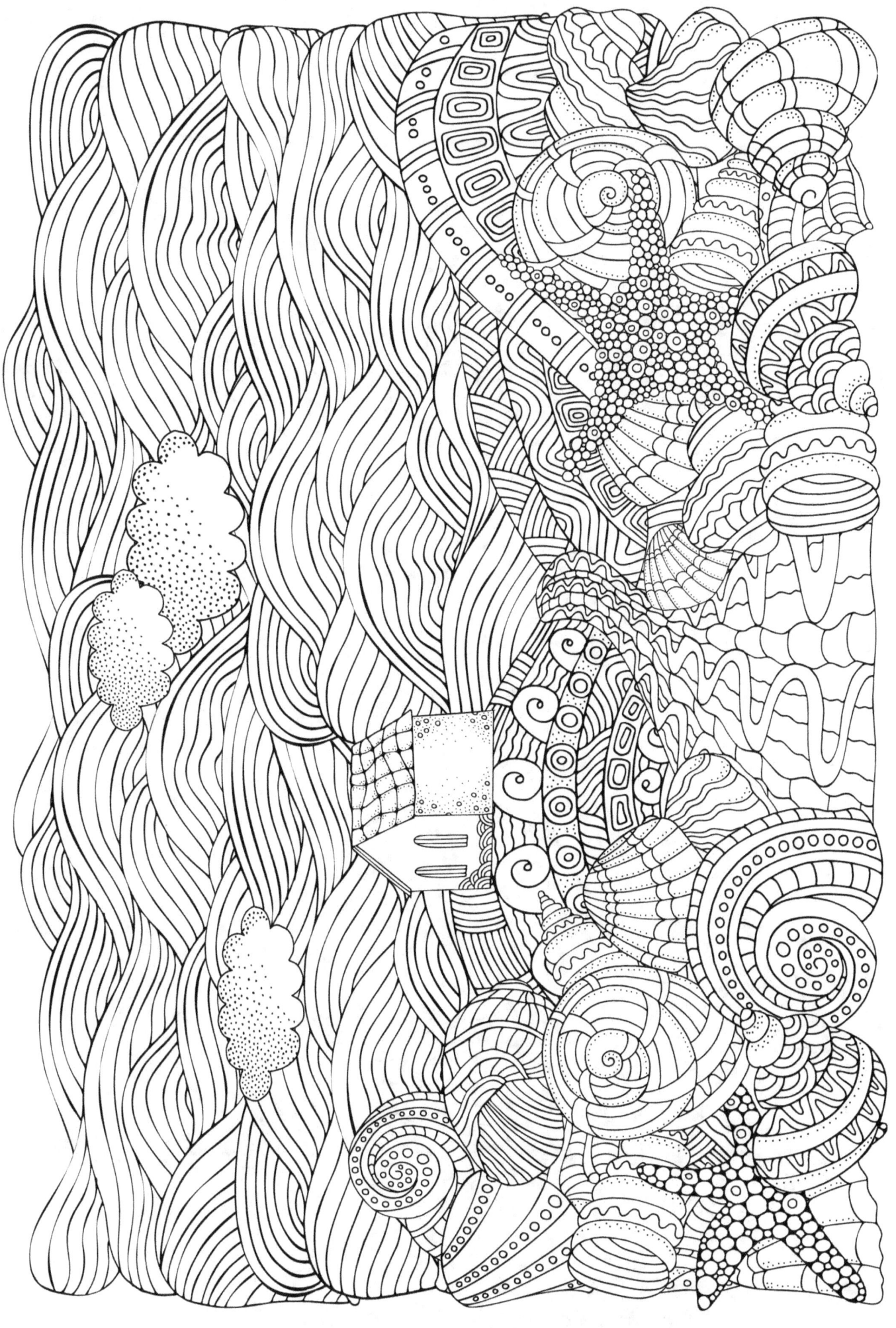

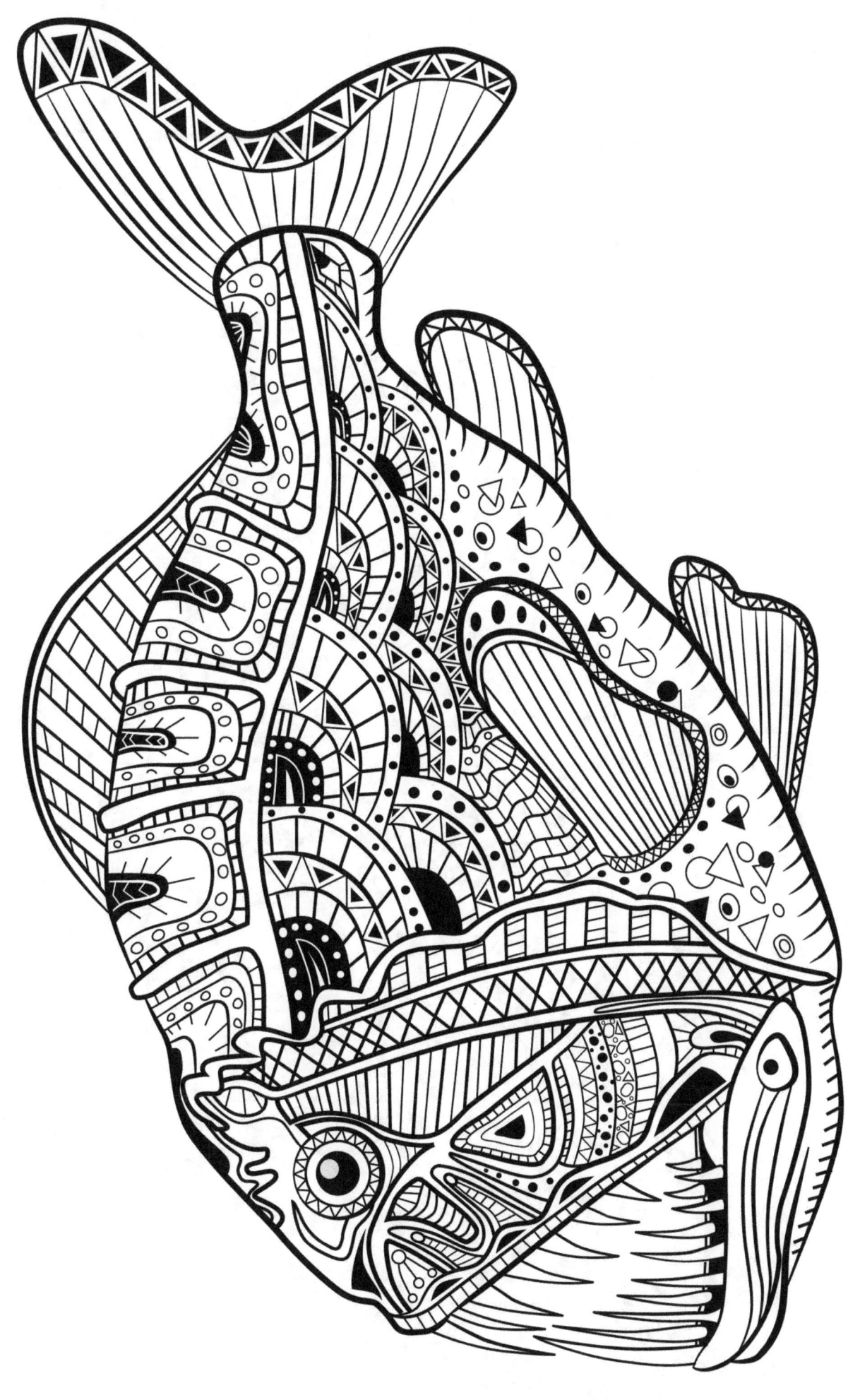

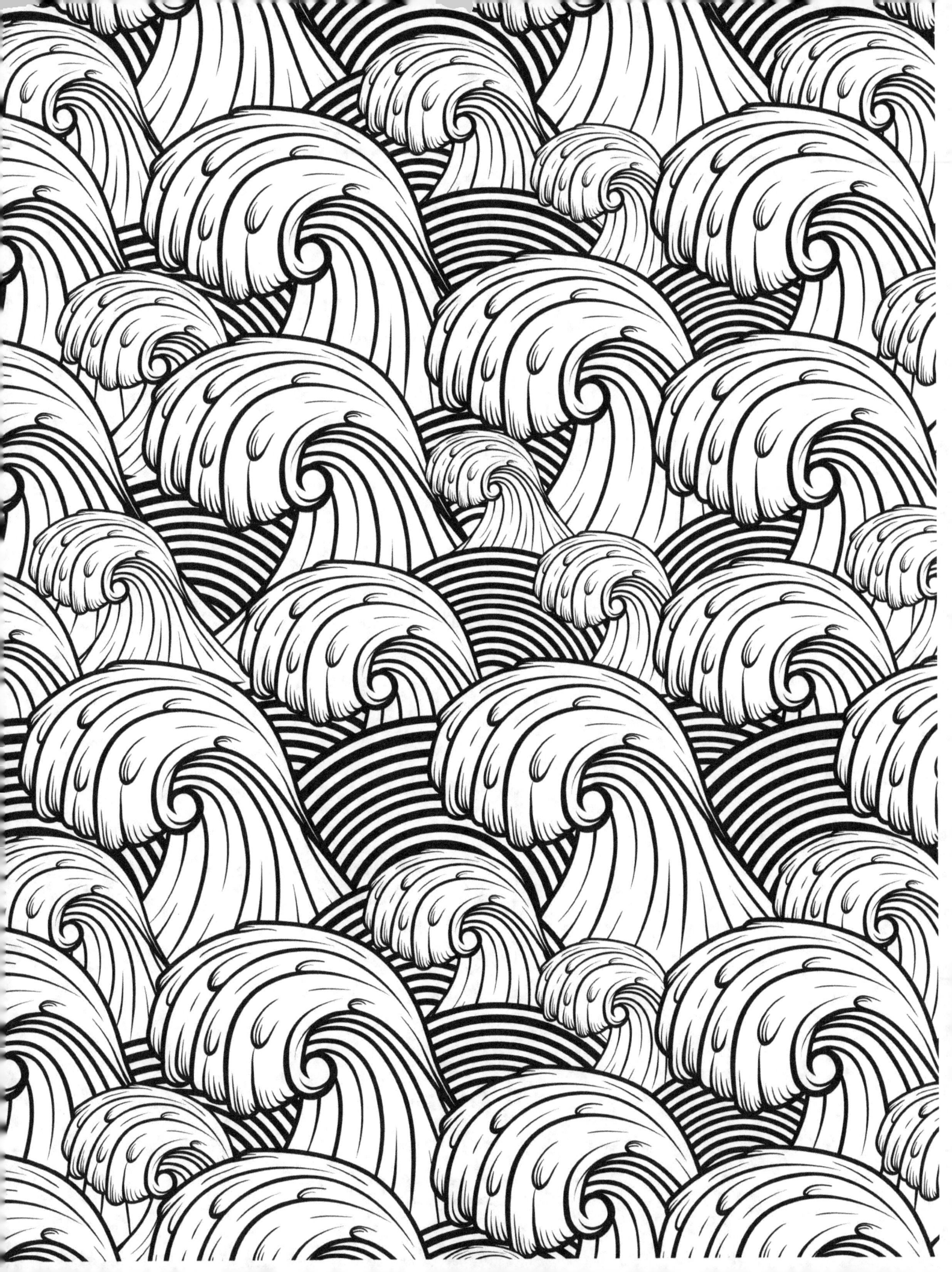

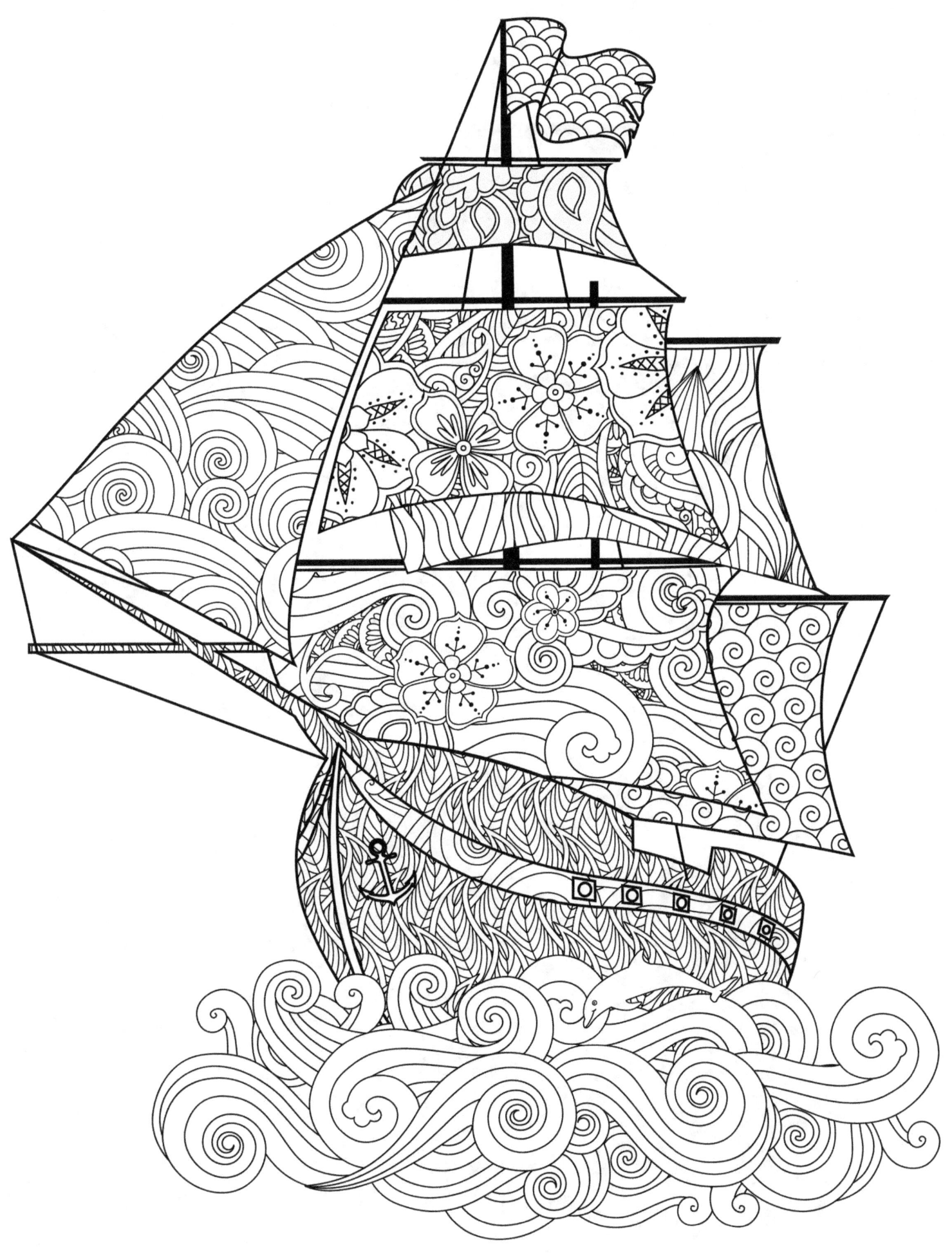

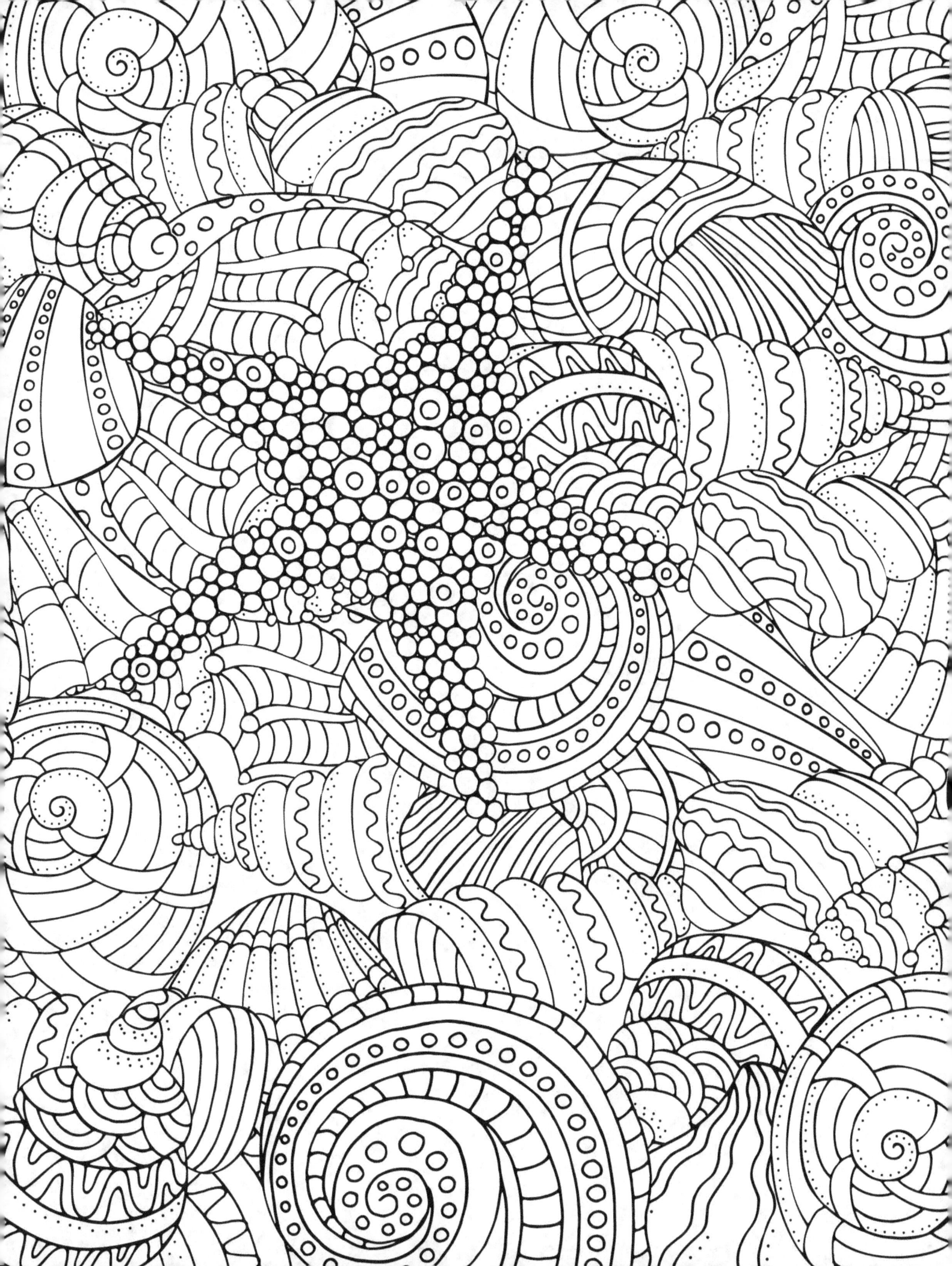

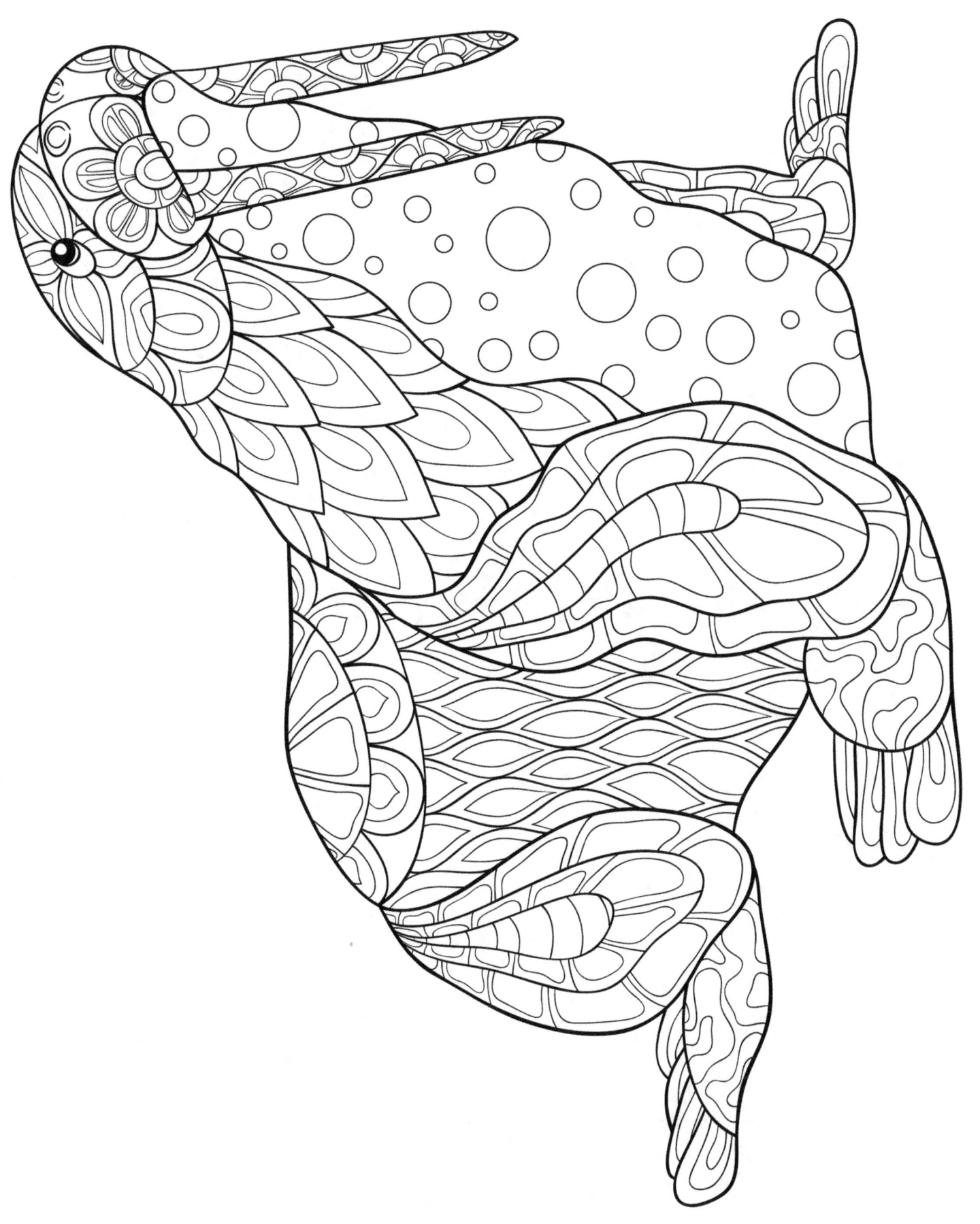

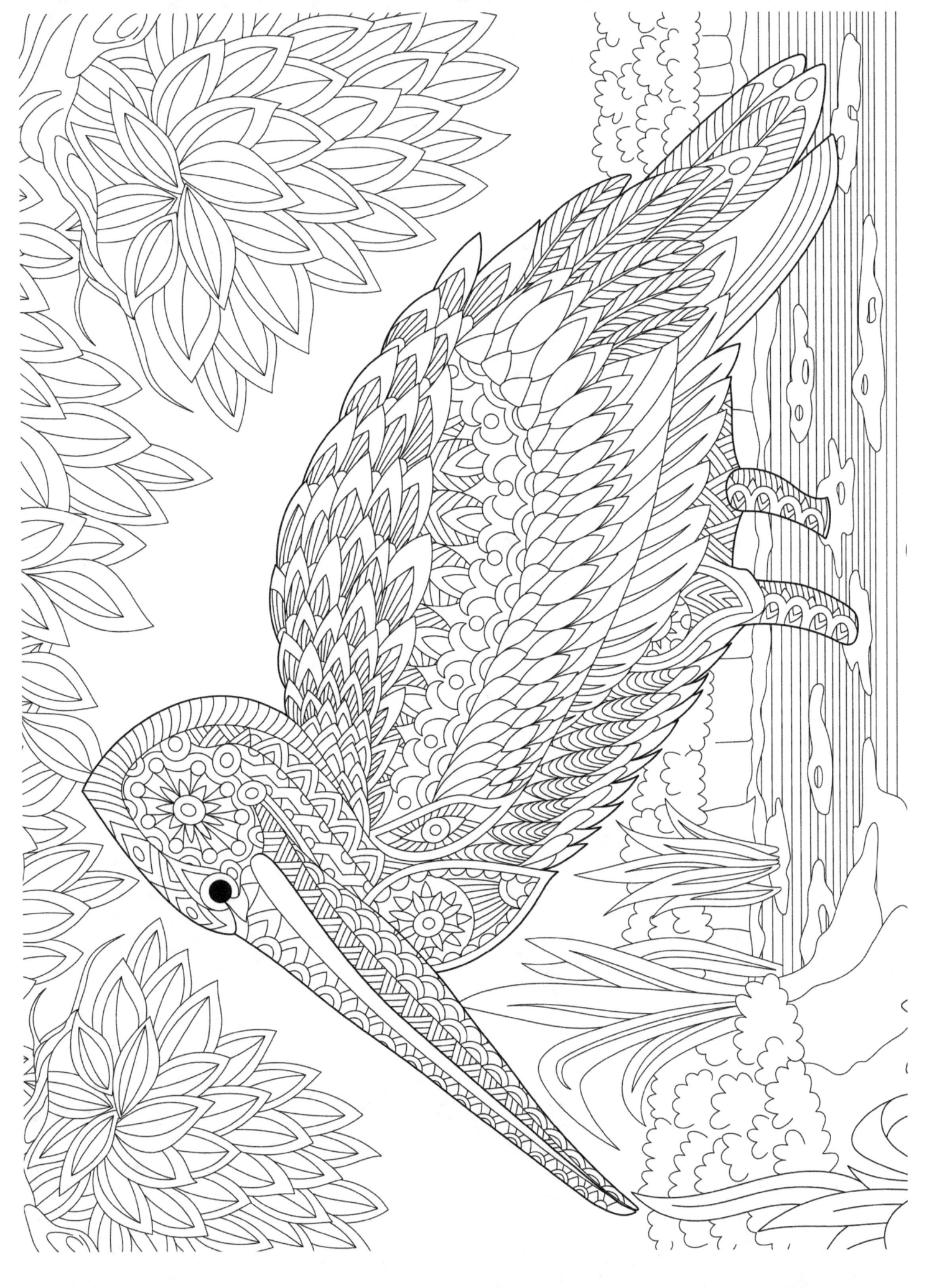

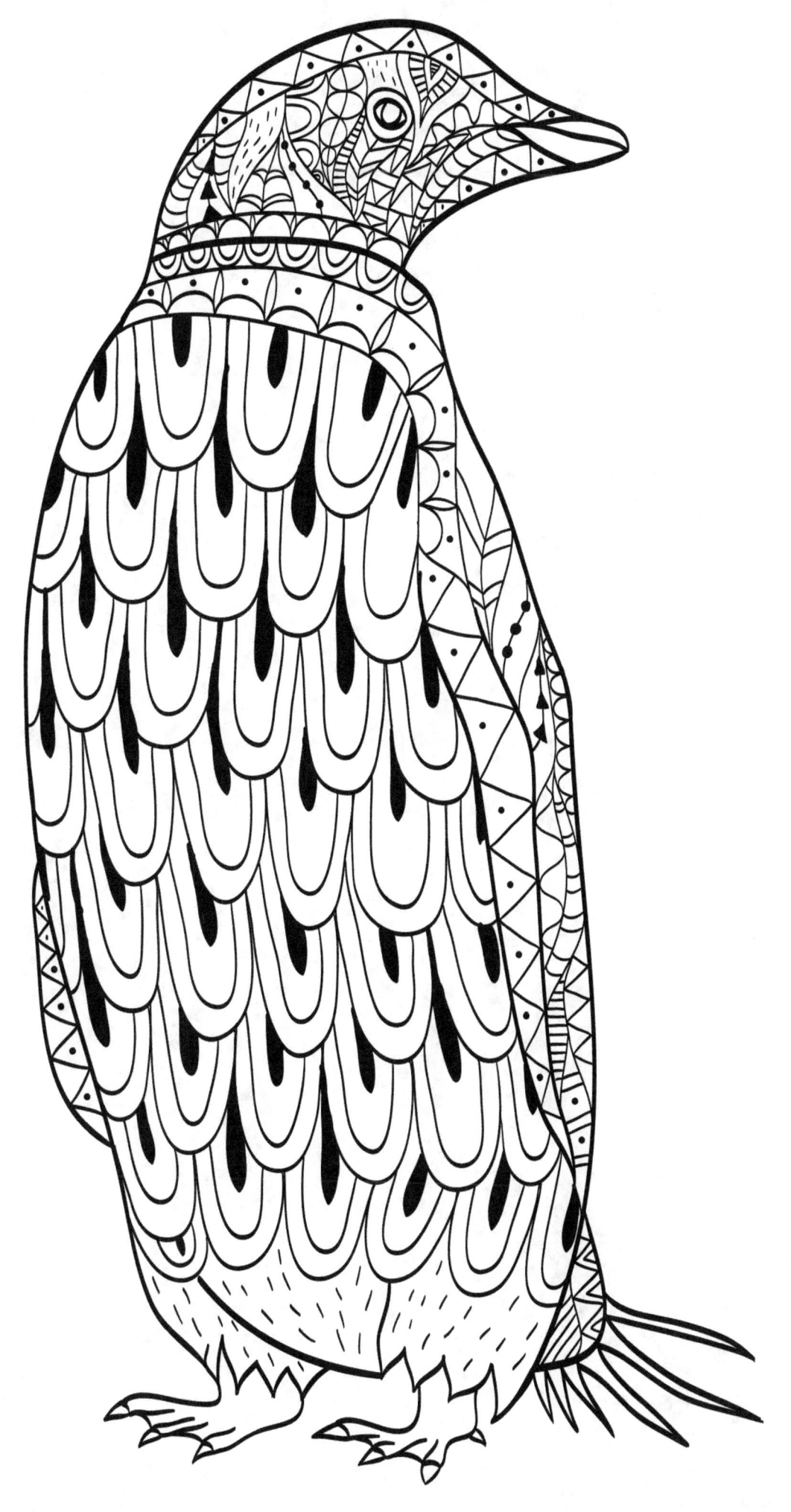

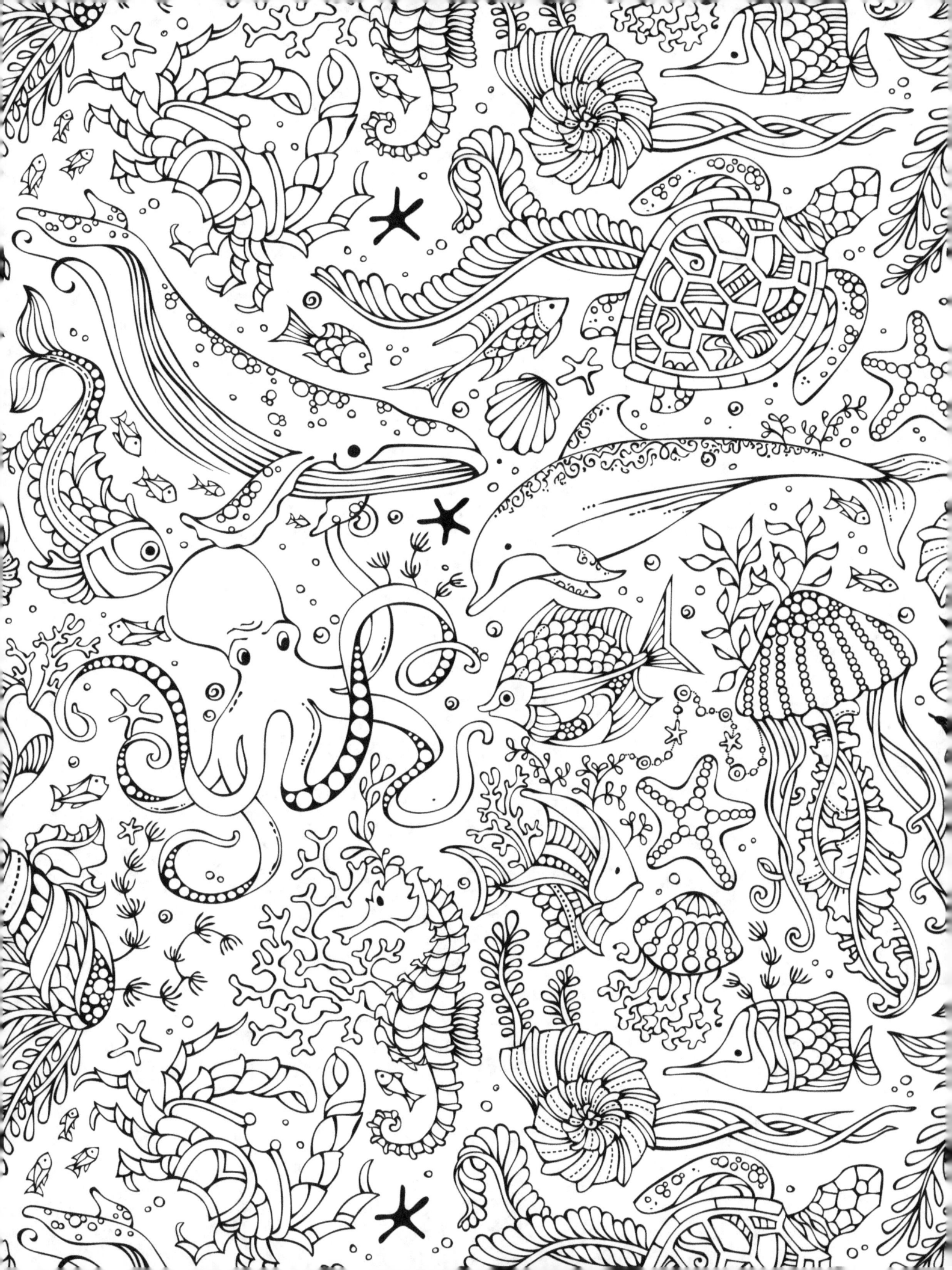

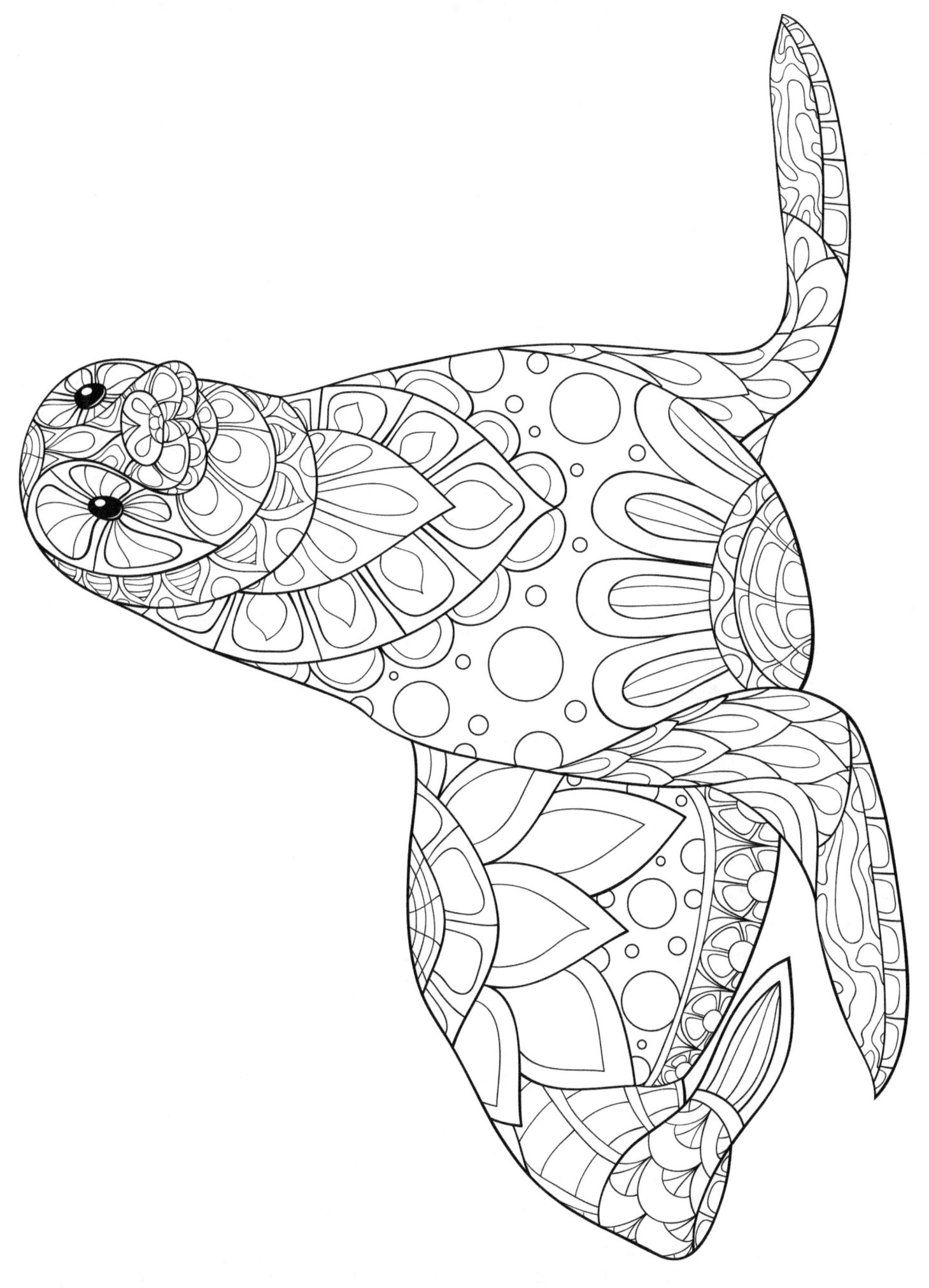

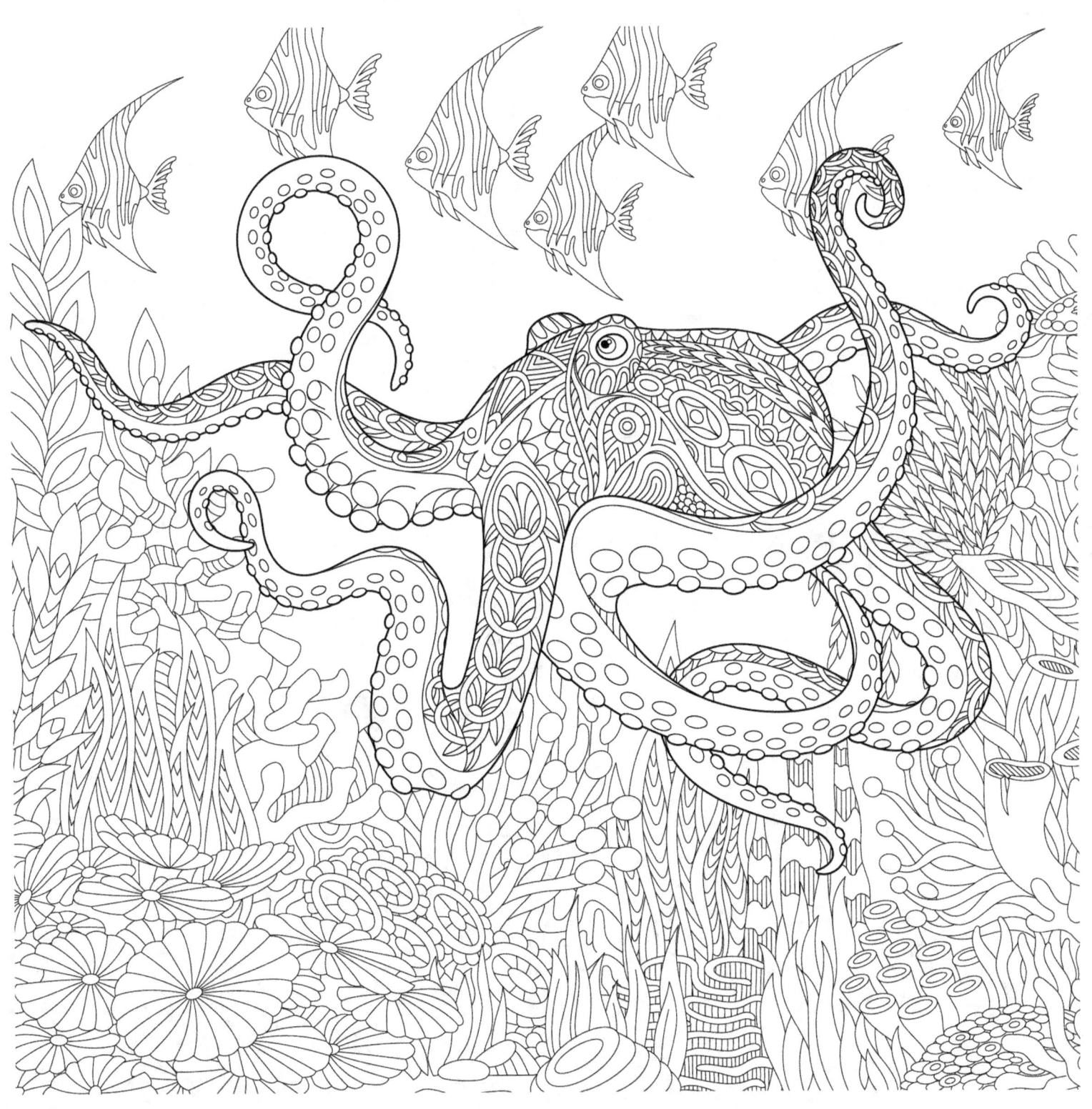

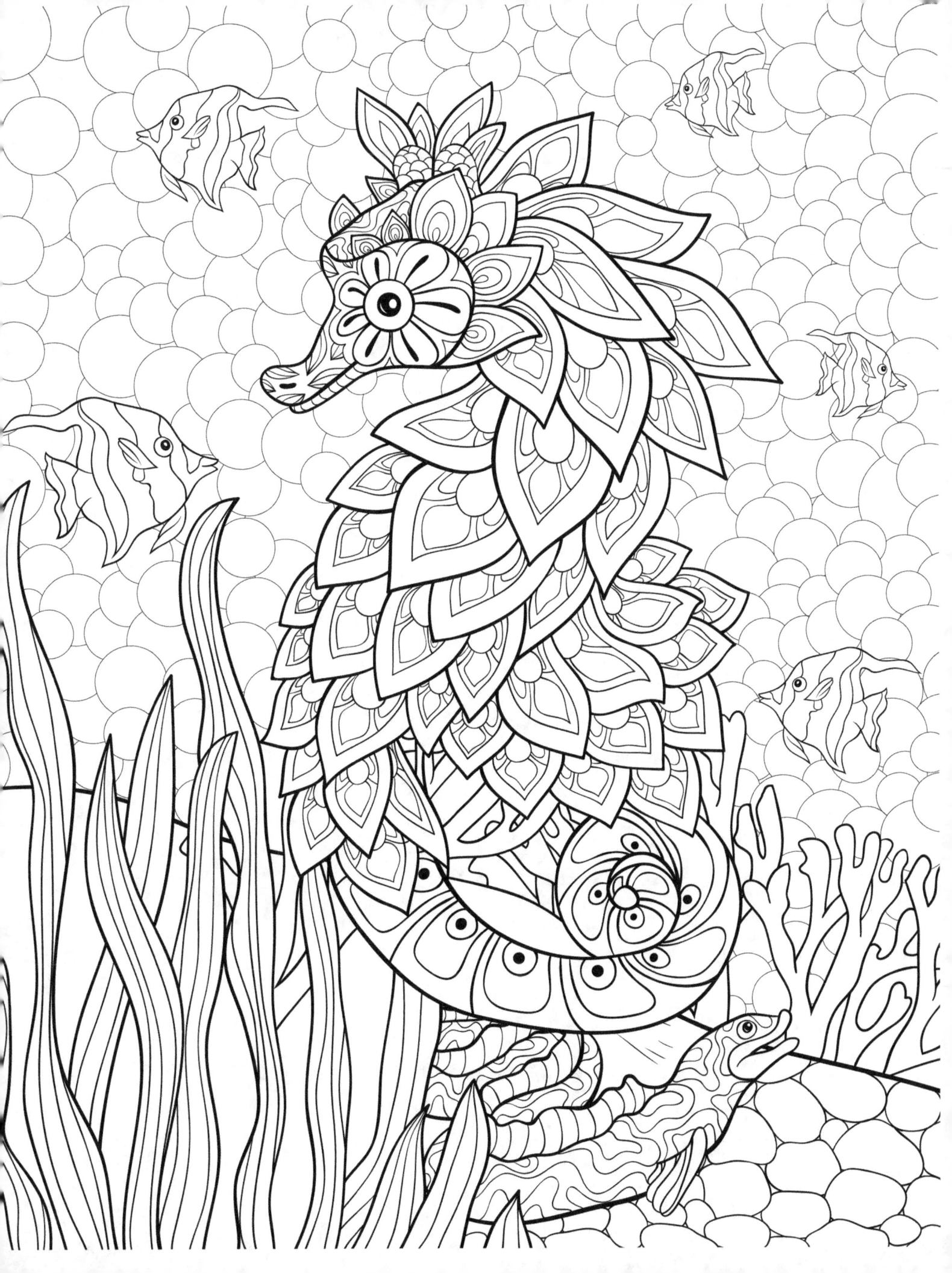

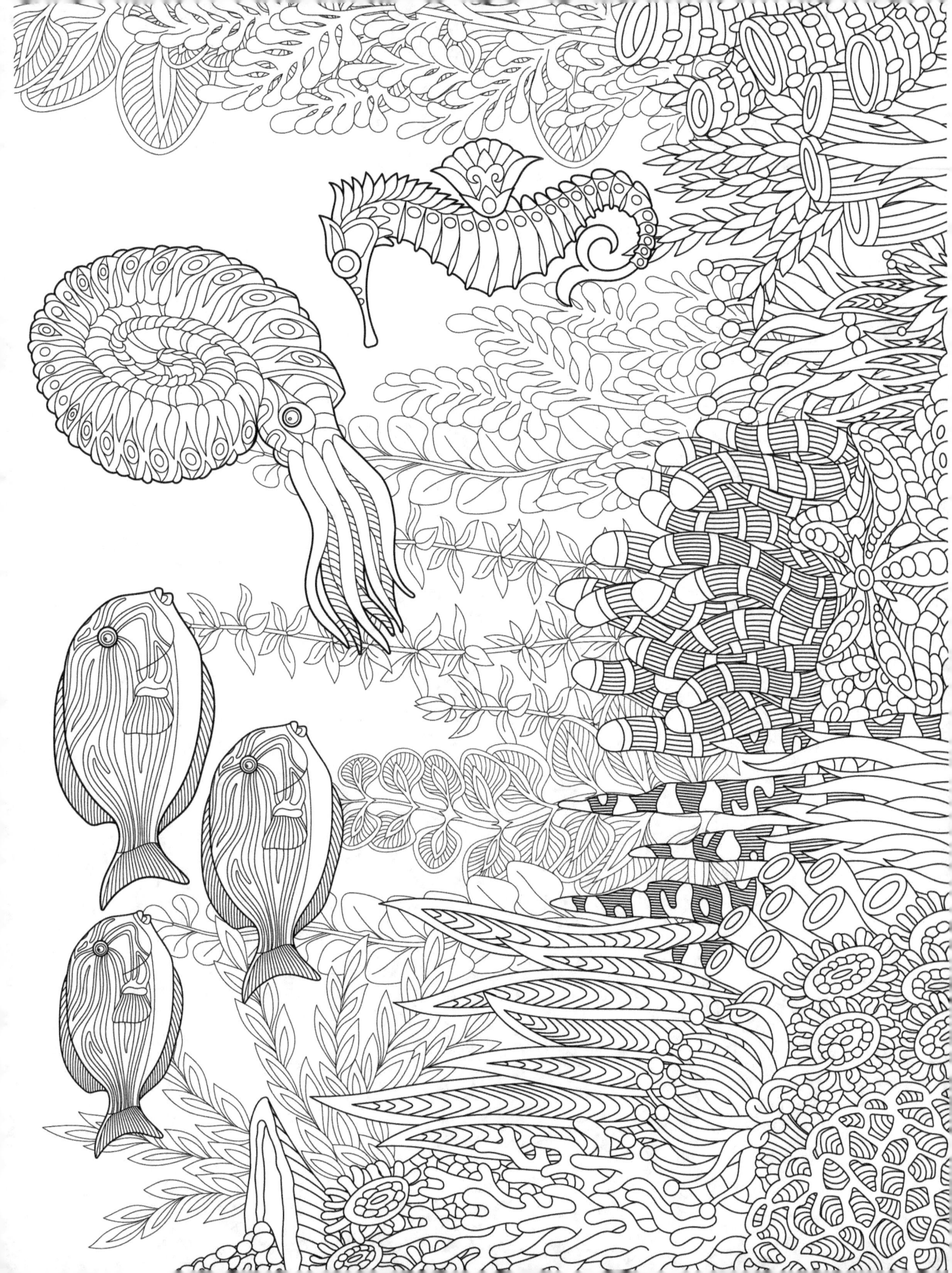

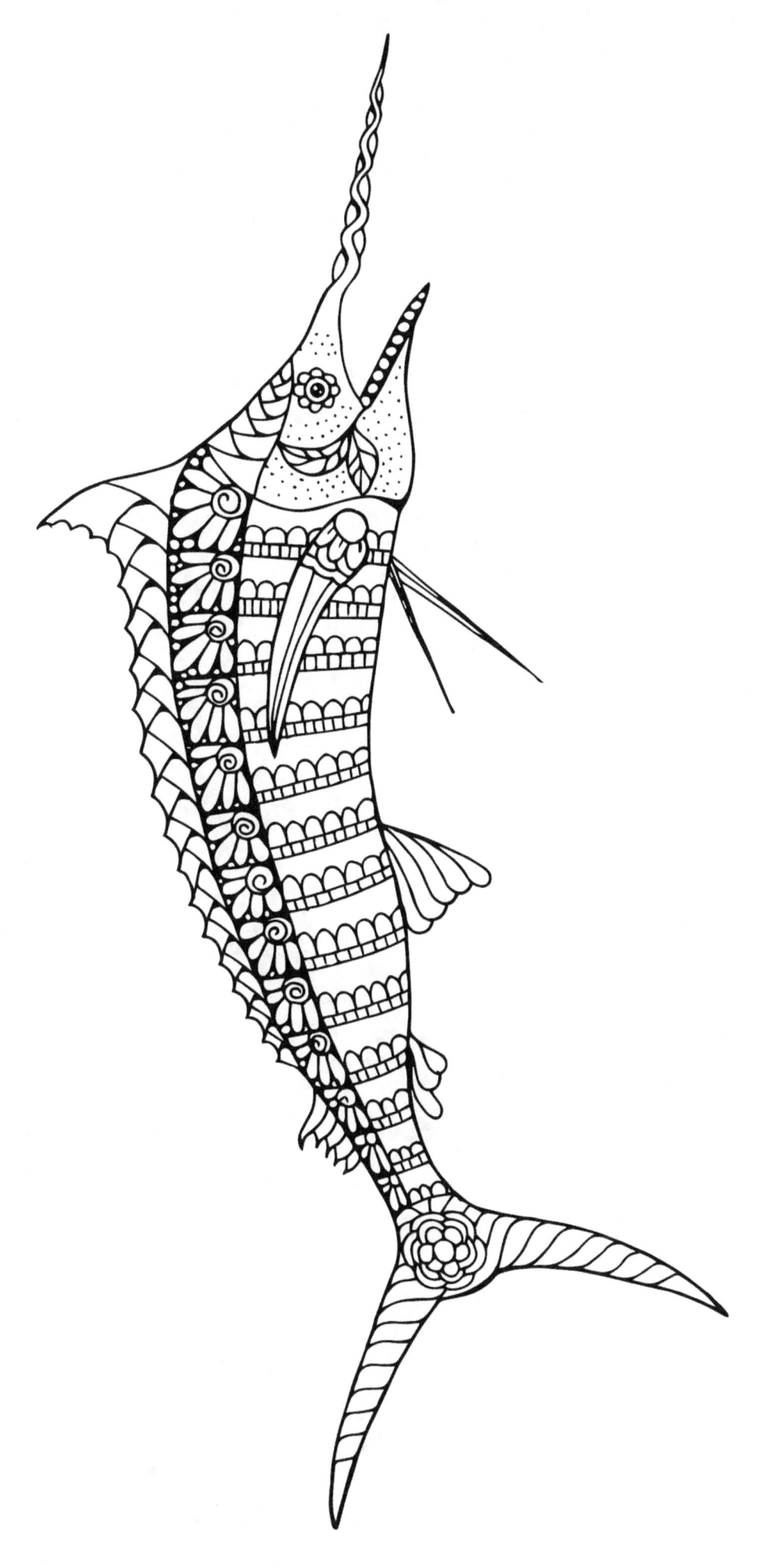

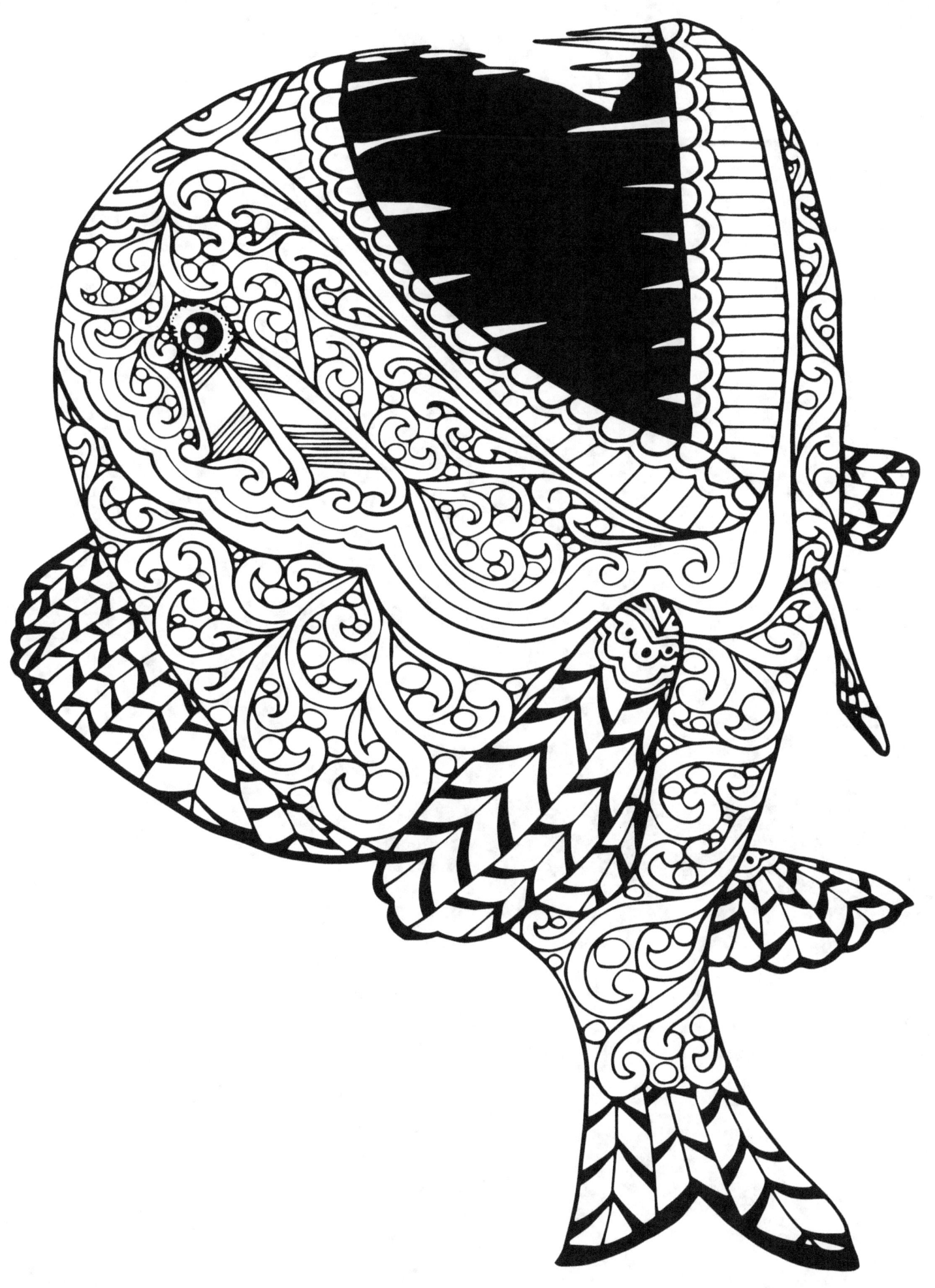

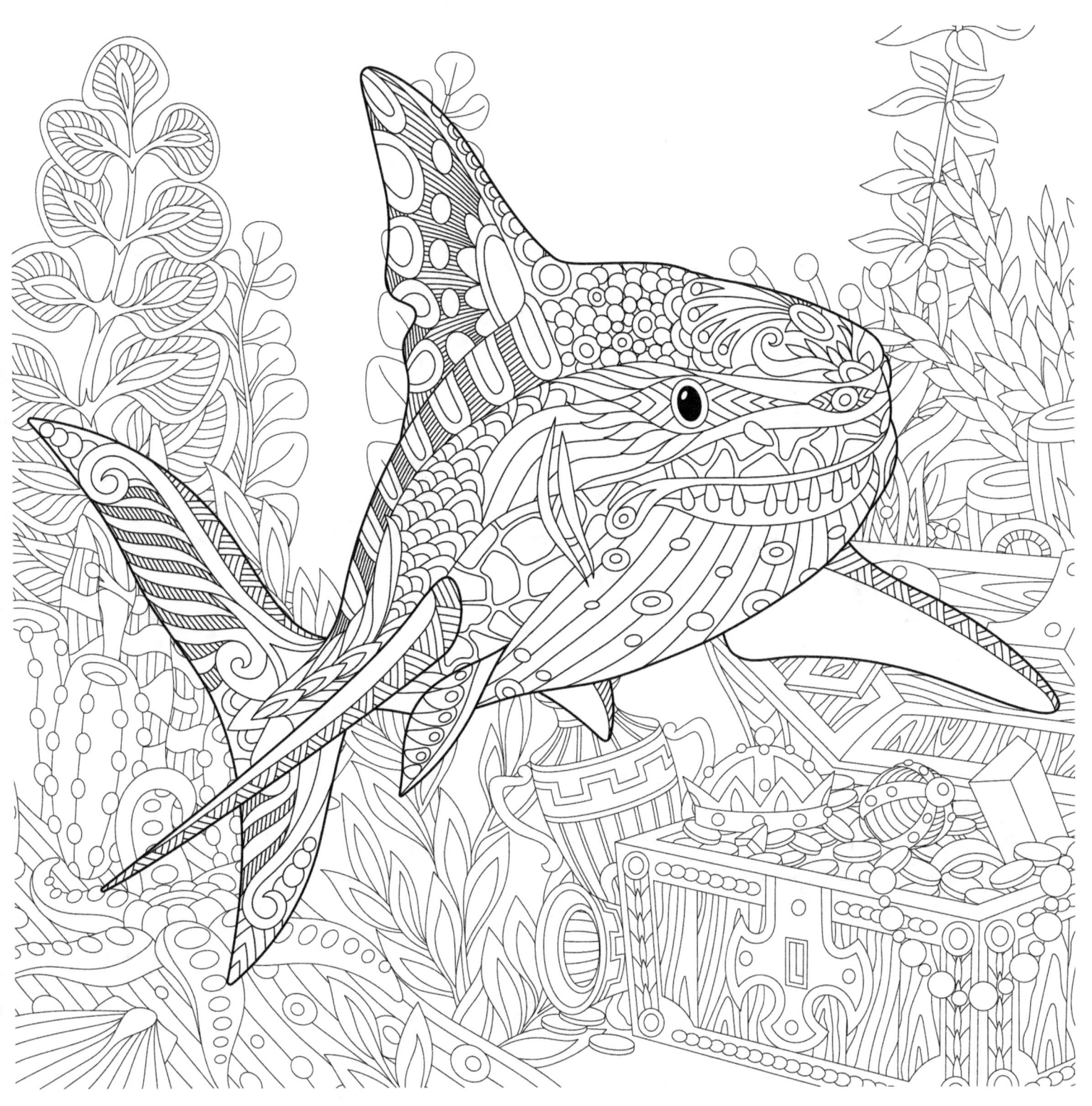

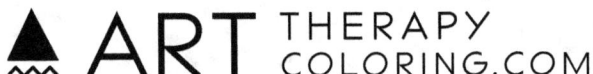

Test Your Colors

Doodles

Best Selling Art Therapy Coloring Books

Coloring Books For Adults:

- Zombie Coloring Book: Black Background
- Butterfly Coloring Book For Adults: Black Background
- Tattoo Coloring Book: Black Background
- Coloring Books for Adults Relaxation: Native American Inspired Designs
- Fishing Coloring Book for Adults: Black Background

Coloring Books For Men:

- Coloring Book for Men: Anti-Stress Designs Vol 1
- Coloring Book For Men: Fishing Designs
- Coloring Book For Men: Tattoo Designs
- Coloring Books for Men: Hunting
- Coloring Book For Men: Biker Designs

Coloring Books For Seniors:

- Coloring Book For Seniors: Nature Designs Vol 1
- Coloring Book For Seniors: Anti-Stress Designs Vol 1
- Coloring Books for Seniors: Relaxing Designs
- Coloring Book For Seniors: Floral Designs Vol 1

Coloring Books For Teens and Tweens:

- Teen Coloring Books For Girls: Vol 1
- Tween Coloring Books For Girls: Cute Animals
- Coloring Books For Teens: Ocean Designs
- Coloring Books for Tweens: Fashion Girls
- Coloring Book for Teens: Anti-Stress Designs Vol 1

Coloring Books For Kids:

- Coloring Books For Girls: Cute Animals
- Horse Coloring Book For Girls
- Coloring Books For Boys: Sharks
- Unicorn Coloring Book for Girls
- Detailed Coloring Books For Kids

Art Therapy Coloring Books

Coloring Books For Tweens

- Animal Coloring Book For Tweens: Zendoodle Designs
- Coloring Book For Tweens: Adorable Animals
- Coloring Book For Tweens: Detailed Animal Designs
- Coloring Book For Tweens: Zendoodle Stress Relief
- Coloring Book For Tweens: Stress Relieving Animals
- Tween Coloring Book: Stress Relieving Designs
- Tween Coloring Book: Wolves, Lions, Tigers
- Tween Coloring Book: Dragon Designs
- Tween Coloring Book: Zendoodle Animals
- Tween Coloring Book: Heart Designs
- Tween Coloring Book: Mermaid & Ocean Designs
- Tween Coloring Book: Ocean, Pirate, Skulls
- Tween Coloring Book: Anti-Stress Travel Designs
- Tween Coloring Book: Ocean Designs Vols. 1–3
- Tween Coloring Book: Stress Relief Vols. 1–2
- Tween Coloring Book: Cute Animal Designs
- Tween Coloring Book For Girls: Calming Stress Relief
- Tween Coloring Book For Girls: Anti-Stress Designs
- Tween Coloring Book For Girls: Meditative Stress Relief
- Coloring Book For Tween Boys: Skulls & More

Coloring Books for Boys :

- Coloring Books For Boys: Animal Designs
- Coloring Books For Boys: Native American Inspired
- Coloring Books For Boys: Ocean Designs
- Coloring Books For Boys: Dragons
- Coloring Books For Boys: Sharks
- Coloring Books For Boys: Wild Animals
- Coloring Books For Boys: Animals
- Dinosaur Coloring Books For Boys: Detailed Designs
- Coloring Books For Teen Boys: Detailed Designs
- Coloring Books For Teen Boys: Detailed Designs: Black Background
- Teen Boys Coloring Book: Animal Designs
- Teen Coloring Books For Boys: Detailed Designs: Black Background

Art Therapy Coloring Books

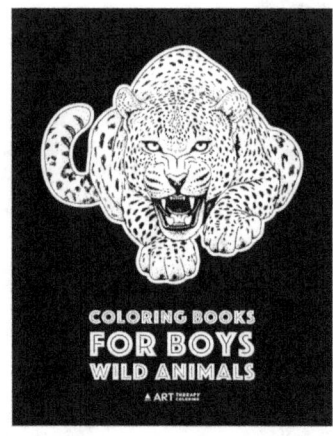

COLORING BOOKS
FOR BOYS
WILD ANIMALS

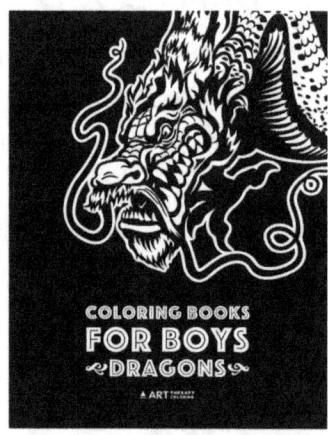

COLORING BOOKS
FOR BOYS
DRAGONS

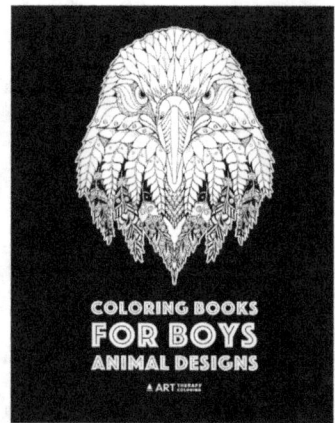

COLORING BOOKS
FOR BOYS
ANIMAL DESIGNS

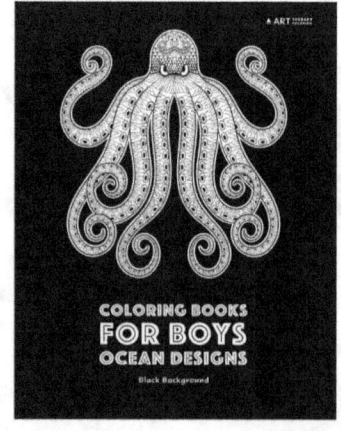

COLORING BOOKS
FOR BOYS
OCEAN DESIGNS
Black Background

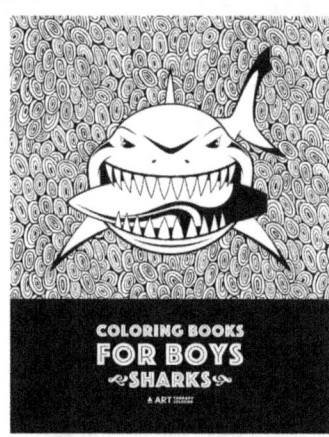

COLORING BOOKS
FOR BOYS
SHARKS

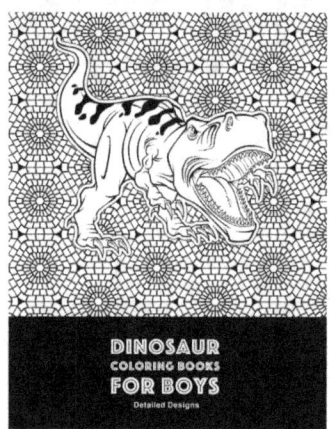

DINOSAUR
COLORING BOOKS
FOR BOYS
Detailed Designs

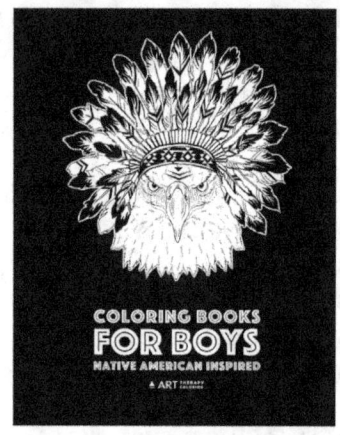

COLORING BOOKS
FOR BOYS
NATIVE AMERICAN INSPIRED

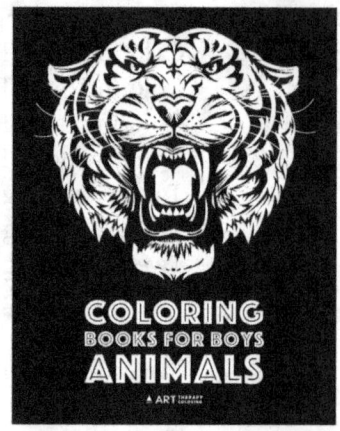

COLORING
BOOKS FOR BOYS
ANIMALS

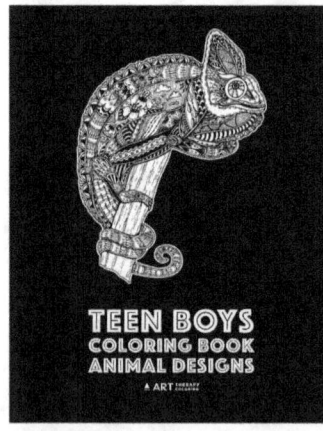

TEEN BOYS
COLORING BOOK
ANIMAL DESIGNS

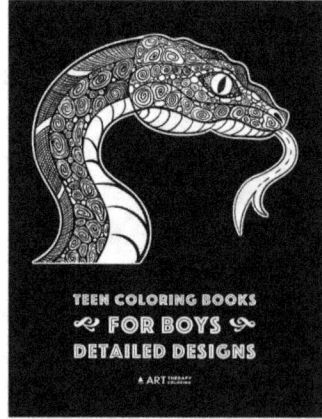

TEEN COLORING BOOKS
FOR BOYS
DETAILED DESIGNS

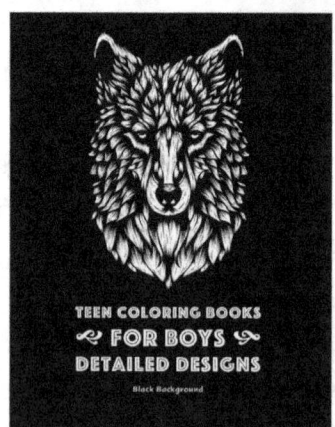

TEEN COLORING BOOKS
FOR BOYS
DETAILED DESIGNS
Black Background

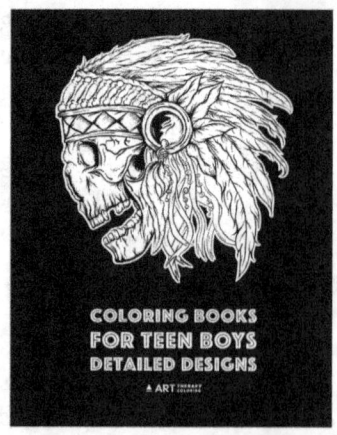

COLORING BOOKS
FOR TEEN BOYS
DETAILED DESIGNS

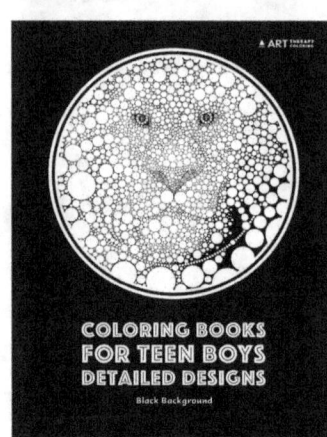

COLORING BOOKS
FOR TEEN BOYS
DETAILED DESIGNS
Black Background

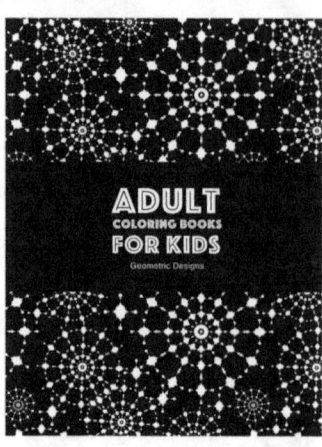

ADULT
COLORING BOOKS
FOR KIDS
Geometric Designs

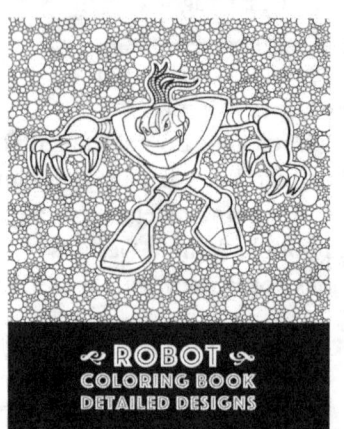

ROBOT
COLORING BOOK
DETAILED DESIGNS

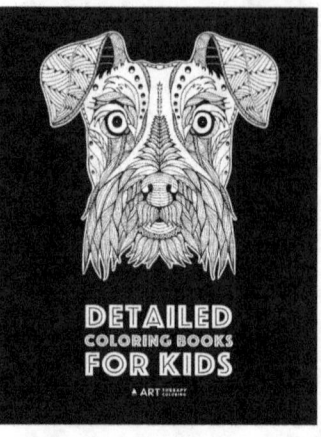

DETAILED
COLORING BOOKS
FOR KIDS

Art Therapy Coloring Books

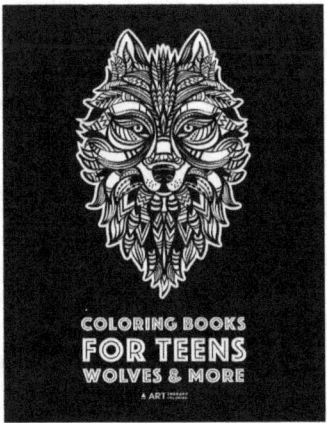

COLORING BOOKS
FOR TEENS
WOLVES & MORE

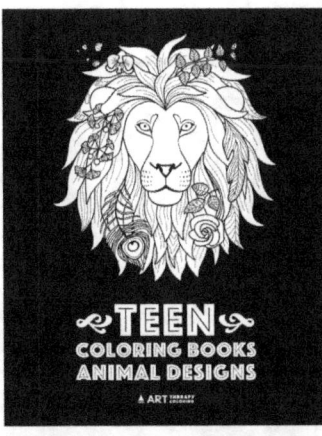

TEEN
COLORING BOOKS
ANIMAL DESIGNS

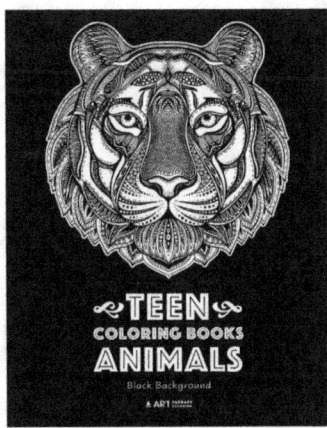

TEEN
COLORING BOOKS
ANIMALS
Black Background

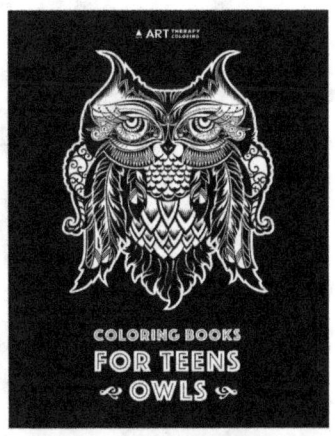

COLORING BOOKS
FOR TEENS
OWLS

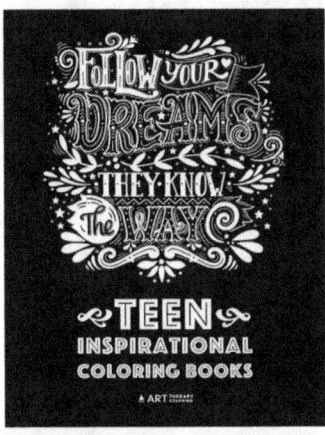

TEEN
INSPIRATIONAL
COLORING BOOKS

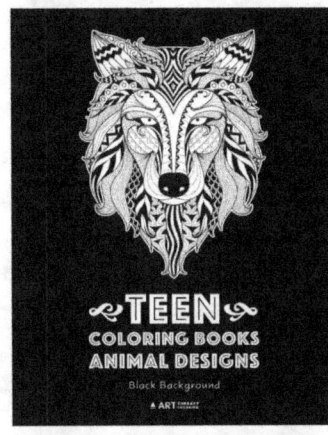

TEEN
COLORING BOOKS
ANIMAL DESIGNS
Black Background

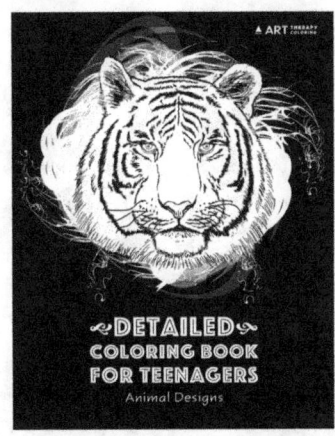

DETAILED
COLORING BOOK
FOR TEENAGERS
Animal Designs

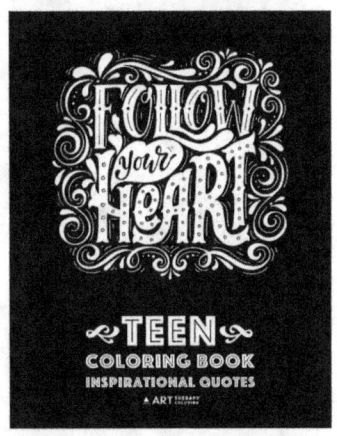

TEEN
COLORING BOOK
INSPIRATIONAL QUOTES

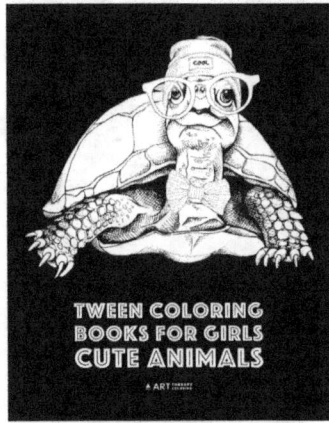

TWEEN COLORING
BOOKS FOR GIRLS
CUTE ANIMALS

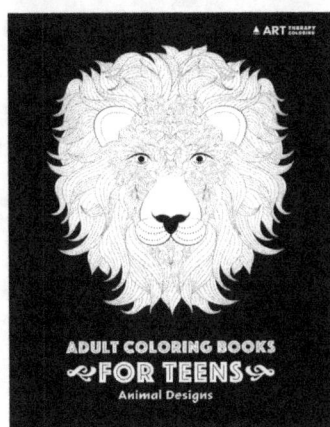

ADULT COLORING BOOKS
FOR TEENS
Animal Designs

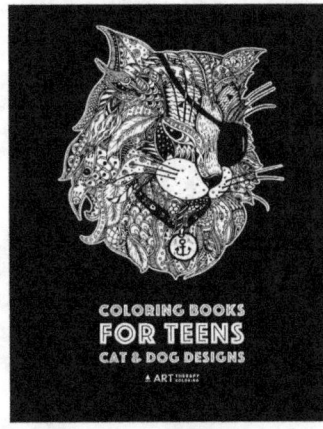

COLORING BOOKS
FOR TEENS
CAT & DOG DESIGNS

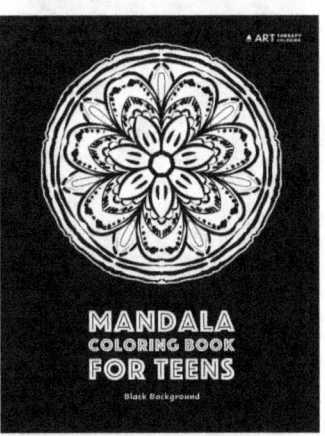

MANDALA
COLORING BOOK
FOR TEENS
Black Background

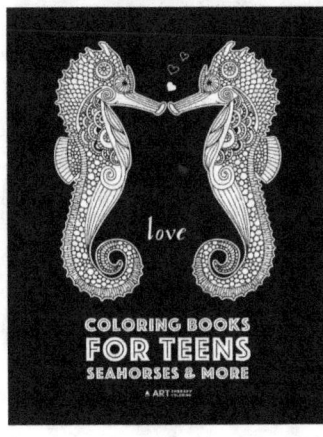

COLORING BOOKS
FOR TEENS
SEAHORSES & MORE

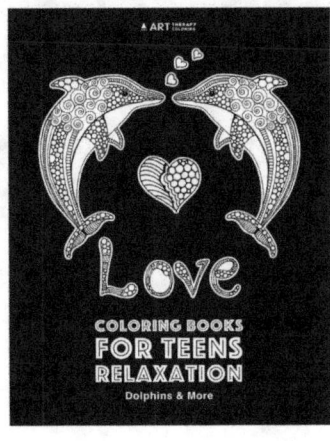

COLORING BOOKS
FOR TEENS
RELAXATION
Dolphins & More

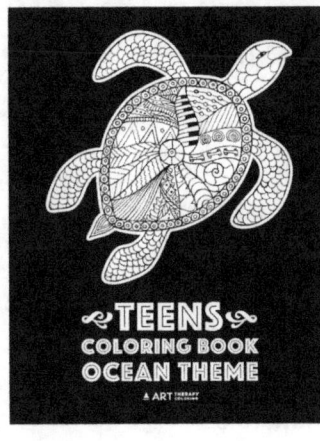

TEENS
COLORING BOOK
OCEAN THEME

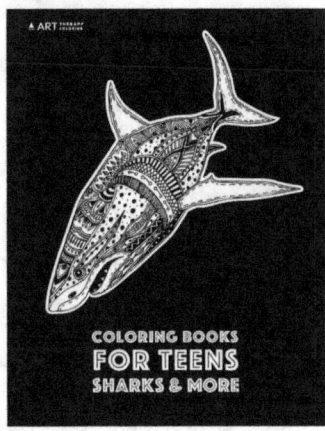

COLORING BOOKS
FOR TEENS
SHARKS & MORE

Coloring Book For Boys
Detailed Ocean Designs

Published by:
Art Therapy Coloring
www.arttherapycoloring.com

Images Under License From Shutterstock

www.ingramcontent.com/pod-product-compliance
Lightning Source LLC
Chambersburg PA
CBHW081346180526
45171CB00006B/607